You and I

Heather Rays

Copyright © 2024 by Heather Rays

All rights reserved.

No portion of this book may be reproduced in any form without written permission from the publisher or author, except as permitted by U.S. copyright law.

Contents

1. ch 1 — 1
2. ch 2 — 8
3. ch 3 — 15
4. ch 4 — 22
5. ch 5 — 27
6. ch 6 — 32
7. ch 7 — 39
8. ch 8 — 45
9. ch 9 — 51
10. ch 10 — 57
11. ch 11 — 64
12. ch 12 — 70
13. ch 13 — 77
14. ch 14 — 84
15. ch 15 — 89

16.	ch 16	93
17.	ch 17	95
18.	ch 18	101
19.	ch 18	114
20.	ch 19	117
21.	ch 20	125
22.	ch 21	134
23.	ch 22	140
24.	ch 23	143
25.	ch 24	153
26.	ch 25	164

ch 1

Anastasia's POV~

I wake up to the sun peeking through the curtains filling my room up with the bright light. My favorite way to wake up. I look over at my phone to see the time. 6 am, just in time. I roll over and get ready for school.

I do my normal routine. Wash my face and brush my teeth. I change into my outfit. Today I was going for a more trendy look. After I change, I apply a little bit of makeup.

(her fit)

I head downstairs and make sure I don't wake up my family. I grab my keys and head to the Petite Cafe. I go here every morning for breakfast and because it's a nice place to study a bit.

When I arrive I walk in and get my everyday order, iced coffee with avocado toast. I sit at a table next to the window and go on my phone.

After about 30 minutes of studying and going on my phone, I see it's already 6:45 am. I get in my car and head to school.

School starts at 8 am but I have to be here and 7 for my daily dose of mean girls. I arrive at school and wait for Meredith and her minions to come.

I sit and draw for a while. All of a sudden.

"Hey misses popular." A voice all too familiar appears at the end of the hallway. Here we go again.

Soon enough, I'm on the floor getting thrown around like a toy.

After about 5 minutes they get bored and walk away. I never tell anyone about this. Why? I don't like when people worry about me.

Going to the bathroom, I clean up my new bruises with a bit of makeup. Strange how they left bigger marks than normal, something probably pissed Meredith off before hand.

I gather my things, walk out the bathroom, and head to my 1st period. I have a little limp because my stomach hurts so bad.

Since it is only 7:15 I have time to do whatever. So I draw. Before I know it, it's 7:45. Many people start to arrive.

"Hey, girl." My Violet says and I jump. "Oh hey, Jesus you almost gave me a heart attack." She laughs at my comment. "Why are you always here so early, what the hell." "I am here early so I get things done Violet I already told you that." "I know I know it's just weird." "Oh shush and get ready for class, the teacher is here."

We pull our supplies out and start doing what the teacher tells us. V (Violet's nickname is V) and I do the work together. I was thinking hard about a question when all of a sudden I heard a big bang that made me jump all the way to Jupiter.

I see Asher in front of the doorway. I guess he opened the door so hard some of the books came off the shelves.

He makes his way to his seat. "Asher, why are you late?" Mr. Jump asks.

I wonder how he always manages to keep is cool when Asher walks in like this.

Instead of answering, Asher rolls his eyes and heads to his seat. Like always, in the back.

"What the hell is his problem?" Violet says annoyed. I just shrug my shoulders.

Mr.Jump sighs in defeat. "Get back to assignment class." All of us do what is told. But Asher just puts his head down and sleeps, I think.

After a long while of silence, the bell rings signaling class is over.

As always everyone gets up in such a hurry.

Violet and I walk out of the classroom. "Hey, Anastasia." "Hey, Ana." "Hey, girly." I am always greeted in the hallways.

I like that I am, it makes me feel special.

"Hey uh Violet I need to get something in my locker will you tell the teacher that when you get there?" "Yeah, of course." I hug her. "Thank you you're the best."

When I got to my locker I pull out some of my new pens.

I walk to the classroom. "Good morning Ana." Misses Flora says to me. "Morning," I say with a smile.

I make my way towards Violet. English is very boring but the teacher is sweet. She once bought me and Violet a whole box of pizza when we came in here for lunch. Crazy right?

Definitely.

A long while has passed and it is now my free period. Violet still has a class. Her free period is the 5th period.

During this time I help around in the office or go to the band room to give the instruments a try.

But today, I decided to just sit on a bench outside and finish up my drawing I was working on a while back.

I finally got the motivation to finish it.

The art represents me. A small girl smiling with tears running down he cheeks.

Meredith has been coming at me for about a year now. It started off with just her but she got Ariana and Sophia to join her. I don't think I will ever find out the reason why.

Class is up which means history. My favorite class. The teacher either sleeps, or makes us watch history videos. Either way no one really pays mind to the class.

...

It's finally lunch.

V and I sit where the rest of the athletic girls sit. I don't like how it's like I am assigned to sit here. But everyone has there group and table here I guess.

"Hey girls!" Tiffany says. "Hey Tiff, hey guys!" I say. Violet gives a smile and a wave.

"I heard Asher got had a long makeout session with a girl before school even started. And I heard he had it here. Whoever that girl is, is lucky." Tiff says.

The rest of the girls agree.

Wait if he had it here, was there any chance he saw what Meredith did? No one is up so early.

I don't understand why they find him attractive. He is mean and arrogant. I just roll my eyes and look at them in disgust.

They all think I'm crazy besides Violet. She hates him. I never knew why, but she does.

So many unanswered questions.

As I am eating, I see Meredith and her group staring me down. I stop everything I am doing and just got up and walked away.

Going to the hallway, I sat in front of my locker and just read a book. That is when I saw Asher slamming his locker and pacing back and forth.

His hands were running through his hair. Even though I wondered why, I decided to mind my own.

As I am walking away, I start to feel guilty. So I walk over to him.

"Hey um.. a-are you okay?" I ask nervously. "What the fuck does it look like little miss perfect." He said through gritted teeth.

All of a sudden I feel sick. I just shake my head and walk away. Like I said, he is rude. I walk into the bathroom and think.

Does everyone truly believe I am perfect? I lost my dad and brother not too long ago. My mom is still grieving even though she tried to pretend she isn't. Meredith pains me for a reason I will never know.

What is perfect? My grades? Those are nothing.

The rest of the school was pretty boring. I got off early. I have fewer classes because I am ahead. So I say bye to V. I thought about telling her the Asher incident but she does not need anymore to worry about.

Every day I get her some goodies for the rest of the school day.

I go to my locker and get my things. After, I head out to my car and start going to the coffee shop. I ordered 2 iced coffees and a cookie for V. Back to the school I go.

Once Violet saw where I went she started jumping up and down like a child. This girl.

'Thank you. You are truly my life savor. My God. My angel.' Violet is obsessed with cookies and coffee. Strange but it's quite funny.

As I was heading home, my mind wandered back to what Asher said. Maybe he was just frustrated? Again, he doesn't know anything about me.

He was nothing but trouble. If I could give him a good slap in the face, I would.

When I arrive its not quite time to eat dinner, so I do homework, change, watch Netflix. Everything a normal teenager would do after school.

But when I started drawing, I got a text.

Unknown- kill yourself.

I was taken back by this comment.

Me- who is this? Unknown- You know me well miss popular ;) Me- Meredith. How the hell did you get my number? Meredith- Secret.

I just set my phone down and thought to myself, I would never think she would go this far to tell me to kill myself.

I was hurt. Why would she say that? We used to be friends. Why did she turn to hate me?

I did not want to be awake so I layed in bed, skipping dinner, and let the darkness take over me.

Make sure to vote! Leave a comment if u like :)Love - steph

ch 2

Anastasia woke up to her mom screaming she is late. She quickly got dressed and did the usual makeup. And ran out the door.

(her fit)

"no no no" she says in worry.

Anastasias POV:

When I arrived I hurried to my 1st period.

"Hi, I am so sorry I am late!" embarrassment filled my voice. "You're never late Ana so I am going to let this pass." Mr.Jump says. "Thank you." I sighed in relief and head to my seat.

Nothing happened that period but Violet kept saying something about a party. I normally never go to parties unless it is like a birthday or something. They're not my type of scene.

"Come on Ana, just one party pleaseee." Jeeslz this girl can't ever take no for an answer.

"V, you know I don't do parties." "I know but please just come to this one, for me? Anastasia next Friday is the biggest party of the year, you have to go!"

She just kept rambling on about how I should go. "I will think about it." I was annoyed at this point. "You said that last time, and before last time, and the time before last time, and the time before-"

"OKAY FINE." I said to satisfy her. She smiled and started jumping up and down.

Looks like I have plans next Friday.

...

Classes are boring as usual. It is now lunchtime. Me and V did not want the school food today because it was this weird lasagna stuff.

We went to In-n-Out. Yum. I just get fries and V gets half of the menu.

We take our food and eat in my car. We see a matte black Lamborghini. My jaw drops. When we see Asher get out of the car with a group of boys, My jaw drop to the floor.

"I adore his car," I say while staring at his car. "Girl, he is from a rich family I am not surprised one bit that he has that car." V says in amusement. "Hm. We should get going, give me your trash so I can throw it away." V gives me her trash and I head back inside. I throw the trash away. When I turn around I bump into someone.

"Oh my god, I am so sorry," embarrassment clear in my voice. "Hey, it's okay, sorry I didn't watch where I was going." I look up to see a very fit teenage boy.

I look around and see Asher and the rest of his friends staring at me. "Nate leave little miss perfect alone." Asher says laughing. "I'll go, sorry for bumping into you." I say while walking away. "Wait what is your name?" Nate asks. "Anastasia," I say quickly.

...

"Ready to go?" V asks when I get in the car. I smile and nod. "What took you so long?" "I had to use the bathroom." "Oh okay."

We arrive at school and head to 4th period. The teacher did not arrive so we all just did our own thing. "V I am going to go home, I don't feel good." "Okay, bye love you." she hugs me and kisses me on the cheek. "Love you."

There was no teacher and this is my last class of the day. So i won't get in trouble.

I hop in my car and drive towards a river I found last year when my brother and dad died. I was going on a run when i found this place.

It has a pretty path that leads you down to it. I go every now and then. It is a nice place to think.

I start walking down the path. I look at my surroundings and take the beautiful sight in. I climb the big rock that overlooks the place. When I reach the top just I lay there and think.

After about an hour, I decide to go to the mall and look around. I look at my phone and check the time. 3:55 pm.

Not too bad, maybe I'll go see a movie or something.

..

Just like I said, I arrive at the movie theater.

I head to the inside to see if they have anything good to see. I look at the selections and see that a new Disney movie is playing.

I buy my ticket then order a drink and kitkats. All of a sudden I hear a little girl's giggling. I turn around to see a teenage boy and a small girl.

She was on top of his shoulders. "ASHY PUT ME DOWN!" She screams while laughing her heart out causing everybody to start smiling. The boy lets her down and starts ticklings her which makes her laugh even harder.

That is when I realized who he was.

Asher.

He is laughing. I have never seen him laugh.

I look at them in awe as it reminds me of how my brother and I used to play.

Tears slip down my face. I snap out of my gaze and wipe off my tears. I turn around and walk into the theater. I sit in the back as usual.

I see Asher walk in with the girl on his back. He looks around for a seat. He sees me and looks at me with a dirty look. I look down.

This is embarrassing._____

We are halfway through the movies and I haven't touched my food. I keep thinking about my dad and Ryder.

FLASHBACK

"He is going to love it, mom." I say as I stare at our masterpiece. "Yes sweetie Ryder will love this." "Ana someone is calling me hold on." I look around as I wait for my mom to get off the call.

All of a sudden i hear her screaming. I run and see her crying on the floor. I run to her and say her name a couple times while shaking her. She won't answer.

"MOM ANSWER ME." i finally scream snapping her out of it. "THEY GOT INTO AN ACCIDENT!" She screams. Hardly able to speak.

I drive my mom and I as fast as i can to the hospital. When we got there the doctors told us the passing of my dad. My mom cries out in pain. All the doctors looked at us with sadness in their eyes. I couldn't feel anything.

My dad was always there for me. He was my best friend. He taught Ryder and I almost everything we need to know. He got me through my first heartbreak, supported me at my first volleyball game, he even was there at my first concert. He was at my first everything when my mom was not. There was nobody as bright as him and Ryder.

But they are gone. And i will never see them, hug them, hear their voices, and laugh with them ever again.

...

My brother has been in a coma for 3 weeks now.

My mom does not talk as much anymore which is understandable.

We drive to the hospital to see my brother. I walk into his room. "Hey buddy." I grab his hand in mine. "Mom and I are not doing good without you and dad. Please keep fighting Ry. We need you. I need you. You are to young to leave. You need more time. I need more time with you." In the middle of speaking to him I heard the most heartbreaking sound.

The flatline.

"HELP, SOMEBODY HELP." I call out. Moments later doctors filled the room. "Ma'am I am going to need you to leave the room." I refused. 2 doctors had to drag me out. I watched as they tried everything to help him. No luck.

My mom came running down the hallways crying. We both watched in horror. A doctor came out.

"I'm sorry, he didn't make it."

* END OF FLASHBACK *

The movie has ended. I didn't realize till the lights we're on. When i snapped out of my gaze once again, i realized i was the only one inside the theater. I gather my things and make my way out.

While walking to my car I see Meredith in the parking lot. "Hey slut!" She calls out. I walk faster. "Listen to me when i talk to you." Meredith is coming closer. I run.

Once I reach my car, I put my things in the passenger seat and drive. I know it will cause me an bigger bruising tomorrow morning, especially because i missed my meet with her this morning, but I don't need anymore bullshit tonight.

My thoughts, my body, everything. I was numb.

Me- hey mom ill be home soon. Love you.Mom- okay. I love you too.

My mom has definitely been doing better since what happened last year. We promised to move forward.

I head over to the river.

My phone read 8:13 pm. It's dark but i won't be long.

I am almost done walking the path. When I get there i thought i heard something. Probably my imagination.

I climb the rock and stare at the sky. The stars are much brighter tonight.

A few moments later, i get up and start heading down. I hear something again. My head darts towards the sound. A figure of a boy is off in the distance. He comes closer and I back up.

Examining the boys face, i finally realized who it was.

It was...

~~~~~~~~~~~~~

AUTHORS NOTE

Who do you think the boy was? Don't forget to vote, thank you!!!

ch 3

"Nate?"

"Holy shit Anastasia you scared the living hell out of me!" He runs his fingers through his hair.

"I was going on a walk and I just saw a path and went down it." He jumps. "Alright well, I have to go, see you around?" I ask.

"Yeah of course, can I get your number before you go?" Nervousness is noticeable in him. I giggle. "Yes, here you go."

After exchanging numbers, I go home.

..

"Hey, mom." "Hey, sweets. Dinner is on the table." "Okay thank you," I say hugging her and kissing her on the cheek.

Breakfast as dinner? Hell yeah, mom.

After dinner, I head upstairs. I put my bags down, strip off my clothes then head to the shower.

the steaming water made me feel relaxed and relieved. I just stand there.

Finally, I wash off. I wrap a towel around my body and hair. "Hm, maybe I should put on a face mask?" after a long while of thinking about it I finally did it.

...

After the face mask and shower, I decided to watch Teen Wolf. Not long after, the clock strikes 12. I am still not tired.

I head downstairs to get a glass of water. "Ana why are you still awake?" my mom scares me half to death. "Jesus mom you scared the shit out of me.

Anyways, I can't sleep and I am thirsty." "Well, you need to sleep because school is tomorrow." "Yeah yeah. Goodnight love ya." "Love you too." And with that, I get water then walk upstairs.

...

I wake up and feel dead. Last night was shitty. Sleep just did not want to happen till 4 in the morning.

It is 5:30 am and since I can't go back to sleep I just get ready. I have an extra 30 minutes to get ready so I find a little more fair outfit to wear for the day.

(Her Outift)

Since the cafe and school are walking distance, I figured I can just walk to school today. I go to the cafe and order my regular order. A chocolate muffin with an iced coffee.

After, I make my way over to the table in front of the window.

(F L A S H B A C K)

I was running home as fast as I could. I was hurt. But at the same time numb.

I run into my house. I scream. My dad came running down the stairs. He looked at me with such sadness and just came up to me and hugged me. No one else showed so I am guessing he was the only one home.

"He cheated dad. I hate him. I never want to see him again. My voice came out a whisper. I ran home so I could hardly breathe. I fell to the floor. My body was too weak to stand. My dad came down with me. We stayed like that till I couldn't cry anymore.

He stood up and held his hand out for me to reach. "I want to take you somewhere so we can talk about it okay?" I nodded in response. I took his hand and he led me to his car.

Only 3 minutes later, we arrive at a small cafe. It was full of flowers and pretty pictures.

"The bathroom is around the corner. Get yourself cleaned up okay?" Again, I nod in response.

I walk in the bathroom and just stare at myself in the mirror. Mascara is smeared all over my eyes, my makeup is ruined and my lipstick is dragged down to my chin. I take a makeup wipe out of my bag and start to wipe off my makeup.

Tears start to fall. Why? How could he this to me? I just ask myself question after question.

After about 10 minutes in the bathroom, I take a deep breath and walk out and see my dad. "There you are, I was beginning to think the boogyman got to ya!" after he said that a smile crept on my lips.

We were in line for about 3 minutes. My dad got hot coffee with a blueberry muffin while I got an iced coffee with a chocolate muffin. "Do you see anywhere to sit?" I shook my head no. "Ah, found one." he began to walk to the direction of the seat. It was a table for two in front of a huge window. We sit down.

He gave me an expectant look. I explained everything to him. I got in 30 seconds without crying. "Take your time Ana, just breath." I took a deep breath and started explaining again. This time holding myself together till the end.

After I was done explaining he just made jokes and we laughed about many things. He even told me when he was in high school he helped mom get through her first heartbreak. I admire how strong their love is for each other. We stayed there for a long time because before we knew it, it was dark out.

"Ana?" I look at him questioningly. "If you need to talk about anything, anything in the world, you come get me okay? You come get me and we will go here. This cafe and we sit at this table. This table will be our table. Just me and you. Okay?" I tear up and just hug him so he knows I agree. "Now no more tears, your brother's birthday is tomorrow and you don't want to be sad on a fun day now do you?" I wipe the tears off my face. "No being sad tomorrow, got it," I said.

"I love you very much cookie. I laugh at the nickname. I have been in love with cookies since I was a baby so he just gave me that nickname. I am surprised he still uses it. 'I love you too dad."

(ENDOFFLASHBACK)

It is now 7 am so I start walking to school. Once I arrive I feel someone pull my hair. Next thing I know I'm on the ground. "Slut."Meredith said. I know I am not a slut so I don't even know why she calls me that.

About 5 minutes pass by and it has been nothing but kicking. Meredith starts stomping on my stomach.

I am begging her to stop because at this point I keep trying to catch a breath but I can't. One last stomp and that one almost sent me breathless.

She stops and I catch a breath. Sophia and Ariana drag me by the hair.

We all freeze when we heard someone slam their locker shut. I silently thank whoever it was because the girls run off. But now i am limping. Not lightly, I mean really limping. It is hard to stand now. How am I supposed to go through the day without anyone noticing?

I walk out of the closet and check my phone. 7:25, crap. People start arriving at 7:30. I try my best to run to the bathroom.

She got some pretty good kicks in today.

I look in the mirror. I have cuts on my stomach. "Shit." is all that came out. I brought extra clothes, since I did, I pulled out a hoodie and put it on to cover myself. Everywhere is bruised badly black and blue.

I put the sweatshirt on when everything stops bleeding. 7:45 my phone read. Stepping out of the bathroom trying to walk properly was not going to happen so my excuse is that I have bad cramps.

I walk out of the bathroom. Wow, the hallway is almost full. "ANA!" I see V across the hall. I wave nervously. She tries to hug me but I flinch. "Whoa, are you okay?" "Yeah just bad cramps." The look she gives me after shows she does not believe me. "I see."

We start to walk to class. I was holding my stomach the whole way there. I scrunch my face when I sit down due to the pain Meredith caused.

I look up and Asher was looking at me with his eyes narrowed. He was wondering about something. My eyes find their way to the front board.

The day goes on and V has not questioned anything. No one has. It is now my free period and I am just sitting outside under a tree. I was deep in thought until I feel my hair being pulled for the 2nd time today.

This school has cameras but no one ever checks them unless they need to.

Instead of them kicking me, Sophia and Ariana keep me up and still while Meredith punches me. 1 punch in the face, 1 on the neck which almost knocked the wind straight out of me, then about a thousand more everywhere else.

"Meredith please stop." I say crying and begging at this point. She keeps going.

Someone hit their locker causing the girls to run off again and leave me on the ground. I pull myself up just to fall again. I limp myself to the nearest bathroom.

I cry when I see what they have done. There is a bruise on my neck and eye but many more on my stomach. The cuts opened and new ones were placed.

Again, I wiped the cuts until they stopped bleeding. I throw my sweatshirt on then go to my locker. I get my makeup from my bag and start covering up the bruises. I look into the mirror in my locker and see that they are pretty covered but I apply a bit more anyways.

I go to the nurse and convince her that I can't stay because I don't feel good and it worked. Since it did, I texted V to tell her I left early. I know I should probably tell V but then she would not leave me alone and she would make sure Meredith and her group stayed away from me.

That is what I want but I won't let V go out of her way to help me just because I'm getting hurt. That is selfish

...

Here I lay just listening to the river. Yeah, I came to the river. Climbing the rock was pretty much impossible so I am on the ground just looking off into the distance.

When about an hour passes by, I decide to go to the cafe.

...

Now I'm sipping on my iced coffee while on my laptop looking at old pictures. I start to cry again. "I need you here dad."

...

It's 7:30 and I am home now. My mom believed my period cramp lie. Since it is almost 8 I figured I should just go to sleep.

AUTHORS NOTE

Sad chap huh :(Poor Ana.

Don't forget to comment and vote!Love- Steph.

ch 4

Asher's POV (surprise!)-

Last night was beyond shitty. Tracy and John would not shut up about my grades. Failing doesn't matter. College gets you nowhere. I think school is pointless. I mean, half the shit they teach you, you don't even need to learn.

"Asher you better get your grades up or else-"

"Jesus Christ, shut the hell up Tracy." They always say or else but nothing else happens. I just get my keys and walk my ass out the door. My little sister Abigail is already sitting in my car.

When I walk in the car and she just giggles at me. "What are you laughing about Munchie?" I say rubbing her head ruining her hair. Munchie is Abigial's nickname because she loves the word munchie. I have no clue why. "Ashy Ashy look I have fruit snacks!" She is a sucker for those.

"Want some?" she asks "You already know I do!" She places one in my mouth then rubs my head and ruins my hair. "Oh no you didn't!" she laughs and I pick her up and start tickling her. "ASHY IS THE TICKLE

MONSTER AHHHHHHH!" I am 100% positive she is the only human in the world that makes me laugh.

After about 5 minutes of ruining each other's hair, I place Abi in her seat. "Ready for the best part?" Her eyes light up and nods her head so fast her head might fall off.

I start the car. "VROOM VROOM" She screams. She's in love with the car and the huge roar that comes with it. "Ready?" She put her arms out and pretends there is a steering wheel in response. I back out of the driveway and speed down the road. "WOOOOOO WE ARE THE FASTEST IN THE WORLD!"

I laugh and head to her school.

We arrive at her school. "Bye-bye Ashy!" She says before hugging and kissing my cheek. "Wait hold on." I fix her hair before she walks out because she really looks like a mess. "Okay, you're all fixed. Have a good day munchkins."

She rubs my hair and ruins it more, then runs out of the car while laughing her ass off. "Oh, you are so on Abigail," I shout at her. She just keeps laughing.

I shake my head and smile. That girl is definitely something.

When I arrive at my school no one is there. I walk in and I could have sworn I heard Meredith. I shake it off and walk to my locker. "Slut." yeah, that is definitely Mere. I wonder who got her panties in a bunch.

"Meredith stop please." A girl faintly said. The voice sounded familiar?

I slam my locker shut so Meredith knows someone is there. I heard them run off. I don't check to see who it was, I just walk the other way.

I walk to the classroom and see that no one is there. "Guess I won't be late today."

An idea slipped to my head and I draw all over Mr. Jump's board. Middle school type of crap but hey, it's funny.

After about 30 minutes, people start to walk in. I just sit there on my phone not caring about anyone in the room.

I could hear laughs at the random shit that was drawn on the board.

I see Meredith and her other two people come in and Mere smirks at me.

Mere is someone I do not like but she is fun to hook up with occasionally and she doesn't leave me alone.

That is when my attention is on a girl who is limping. There was a hoodie on her head so I couldn't see who is was.

I just shrug it off.

Class begins and I groan. The teacher glares at me and I give my signature smirk. He spent most of the period lecturing us to not write on his board.

My eyes start to wander around the room. I see Mere and her little minions snickering at someone. I trail my eyes to what they are laughing at. Then I realize who the limping girl is.

I see Anastasia got herself caught up with Meredith.

She sees me looking at her, then looks down. Weird.

The class is over and now is half the school's free period. Mine is during 5th and I hate it but I skip anyway.

I was walking down the hall next to the door outside. I hear the same voice telling Mere to stop. Mere can't ever catch a breath.

I slam on the locker hard enough for them to hear then no sound of the girl begging is left, which means Meredith and the others left.

But the voice sounded so familiar.

The day goes by and I am at a pizza place with Nate and the others.

When that ends, I pick Abi up. I decided to go to the cafe my mom used to take us. "Wow, this place never changed," I say as I walk in. I look around and take in the surroundings.

"How come I've never seen this place before?" Abi asks. "You have munchkins, but you were just a baby."

We get to the front counter and i ordered a chocolate muffin for Abi. We find a seat then sit. "Yummy!" I smile at her. "Your hair is still messy Ashy!" She giggles causing people to turn and look at her in awe.

In the middle of a conversation with abi see an all to familiar face. Anastasia. It looks like she is crying from something she sees on her laptop. "I need you here dad." Is all she says before she leaves.

What the hell. What happened to her dad?

I drive me and Abigail home. Abi wanted to watch Moana in my room so i let her. I have my arms around her while she is watching the tv screen. I stare at the ceiling wondering why Anastasia said what she said.

Do I care? I don't. I am just being nosy.

Eventually Abigail falls asleep. i kiss her on the cheek. "Good night munchkins." After, I let my mind go crazy till I doze off into the blackness.

AUTHORS NOTE

Ana left Asher wondering! What do you think Asher will do if he finds out she is the familiar voice she is hearing?

Don't forget to leave a comment and vote! Thank you loves:)

ch 5

ANASTASIA'S POV-

The first thing I did when I woke up was put makeup on to cover the bruises on my neck and eye. But hey, its the weekend finally.

"Morning Ana." my mom greets me when I walk downstairs. "Morning mom." "Any plans this weekend?" "Nope, I don't think so." We just sit there eating our breakfast.

"So mom, there is a party on Friday-"

"Yes you can go and I know I can't stop you from drinking and doing other things so be careful is all I am going to tell you, okay?"

I was taken back by her comment. I thought she was going to say no.

"Well you know I won't drink mom." I refuse to taste alcohol. Dad and Ryder died from a drunk driver.

Mom decided since I don't have plans, we should go shopping. I quickly change into something other than sweats and a t-shirt.

(HEROUTFIT)

We are now in Urban Outfitters and I picked out a few cute clothes. My mom got a fuzzy coat which is funny because she has like 100 of them.

After going to almost every store in the mall, we go to Menchie's. I love this place.

"You know Ana, I see you have a little limp. May I ask why?"

I choke on my frozen yogurt for a second. "Oh.. Uh.. um, I have really bad cramps." I said in the most honest voice I could make. She looks at me the way V did. She nodded but I know her and she does not believe me.

When we finish we go to a couple more stores. My mom bumps into this girl and they start talking. Since she forgot I was here, I start to wander off in the store. My attention is suddenly all over this outfit I saw that was perfect for the party. I hate them but when I go to one, I put in the effort for it.

When I buy it I go back to Mom. She is still talking to the girl. "Can we go now?" I said in unison with someone else. I look to see who it is.

ASHER?

ASHER'S POV-

Tracy decided to make Abigail and I to the mall for stupid bonding time. I only went because Abi wanted to.

When we arrive we just go in and out of a million different stores. I bought Abigail some things she wanted. I am carrying her bags with 1 hand and her little hand is in the other.

The day goes by and we all start to get bored. Tracy went into a store that did not interest Abi and I so we went to the toy store.

After about 30 minutes Abigail got tired as hell. So i carry her toys and bag. She is on my back with her head sound asleep on my shoulders.

"Can we go now?" Me and someone else said at the same time. I look to see who it is.

ANASTASIA?

I give her the best death glare i possible could. Then i notice a little dark spot around her face and a little darkness on her neck.

Are those bruises?

Before i could see for sure, she puts her head down and asks for the restroom. What the hell.

ANASTASIA'S POV-

He sees me. I gave him my best death glare and he gave me his but also looked at me observently.

Could he see the bruises? I put my head down.

"Mom I am going to the restroom really quick I need to fix something."

I see that the makeup around the bruises was slowly wiping off which means.. he. probably. saw. the. bruises. 'Shit shit shit shit shit. Curse this hot weather.' I cover the bruises again and go out.

"Let's go." I told my mom in a rush. I did not want him to see me.

I basically dragged my mom out of there, but i did not want to be anywhere near Asher. 'I'm sorry mom.' I say.

"Tell me why you and that boy looked at each other like you both wanted to kill each other." My head goes down and i just shrug and get in the car.

The whole car ride home was silent. When we arrive to the house, I give my mom a hug and kiss her on the cheek. "Thank you for today, i had fun." She smiled and nodded.

I head upstairs and changed into shorts and a sports bra. My pencil glides on the paper. What i am drawing? I have no idea. My imaginitation is let wild.

After a while, my drawing is finished. It's an eyeball with a forest inside.

There was a knock on my door.

"Open it." I say. Mom walks through the door. "Dinner is ready." She says softly. "Okay."

She sits on my bed. "Your drawing...what is the meaning behind it?" "Um, if i am being completely honest..i have no idea. I just decided to let my imagination run wild." I said with a small chuckle.

Her eyes held worry. "Mom, I'm okay." She just nodded. "Ready to eat?" She asks. "Yeah."

Dinner has been awkward. It was silent the whole time. Weird. We shared small glances, but that was it.

...

I'm in bed thinking of what I should do since tomorrow is Sunday. Ask V to hang? Nah she will nag me about the stupid party. Go to the mall? Already have today.

After a long while of thinking, I finally decide what I will be doing tomorrow. Then sleep takes over.

AUTHOR'S NOTE

Oh no Asher saw that Anastasia might have bruises on her!

Hey guys! Hope yall enjoyed the chapter<3If there are any mistakes please kindly comment, i will fix them.

Please don't forget to vote!

ch 6

Anastasia's POV-

My morning was like every other morning. I look at all my bruises and it looks like most of them are fading away but the one on my neck and face are not, and they are the 2 I need to go the most. Life is nice, isn't it?

My limp is finally gone.

I look at myself in the mirror one last time. "Not bad," I say to myself.

I grab my keys and tell my mom bye then walk out the door. My plans today were at the river but before I drive there I took a quick selfie and posted it on Instagram.

I go to the grocery store first so I can buy some food before I go to the river.

I arrive at the river and walk down the trail.

"Nate, hi!" I exclaim. "Ana, what's up?" "Ah nothing but, I got the goods," I said pulling things out of the bags.

Nate grabs the KitKat so fast. "Whoa, looks like we are both suckers for KitKats."

"As you can see," He said with a slight blush. "I have an addiction." I let out a chuckle.

Yeah, Nate is my plan for today. he seemed pretty cool so I thought it would be fun to get to know him more.

We talked about the dumbest shit. "Wanna go for a swim?"

He asks. I look at him seeing if he was serious. Turns out he was because he started taking his clothes off.

Awe why the heck not? I proceed to strip my clothes off leaving me in only panties and a bra.

"WHOEVER IS LAST TO THE WATER BUYS THE WINNER A BOX OF PIZZA!" I yell. We both start running but I won.

"Awe man, do I really have to?" He asks. "Yes dumbass." I splash him with water. He mimics my moves. Soon enough we are both just splashing each other.

We are laying down in the water. "How did you find this place?" I was silent for a moment. I never talk to anyone about this.

Violet acts like she is walking on eggshells when it comes to this topic so I never talk about it. I need to talk about it to someone so I decided well I could talk to Nate about it.

"Well...when my Dad and my little brother, Ryder, died in a car accident last year, I was caught up in all the emotion and decided to just run until I couldn't anymore. When my legs gave out, it was in front of the trail that leads to this river. Me being the curious person I was, I decided to go down the trail. Ever since then, this place has become my favorite place."

He just sat there with disbelief.

"Wow Ana, who knew someone as positive as you could go through such a big thing like that. You must adore so much to tell me." He says with a wink.

Oh my, "Don't get cocky now." I said with a laugh. We dried ourselves off, put our clothes back on, and took a spin to a small ice cream truck down the treat where he lived.

"The man who works here, his name is Jack, he is cool. You will like him." I just smile.

"Nate, what's up my man?" I am assuming Jack said.

He was a tall muscular man who had the brightest smile. "Jack, I would like you to meet Anastasia Smith." "Ah, I've heard of you. I am sorry about what happened last year. Now, what can I get y'all?"

We ordered our ice cream. "How much? I ask. he nodded no "Uh uh uh young girl, I think Nate should pay. Actually, I'll let you both get a pass, have a nice day." I also nod my head no "Ah ah ah." I say handing him a 50 dollar bill. "Now, you have a nice day. Keep the change." I wink, grab Nate's arm and we make our way my car.

"Well that was nice of you Ana."

'I am awesome aren't I?' I tell him. He laughs 'You are definitely something else.'

We head to the mall. Our last stop of the day is the movies. We went to watch 'It Chapter Two' so we can scare ourselves.

When we arrive we fall in line. My luck, I see Asher and Meredith fall in behind us. Meredith and Asher see us.

They give us a 'what the hell' look. I am guessing it is because Nate and I were together right now.

"Nate can you get my ticket please, I need to go to the restroom real quick."

"Yeah, sure ill pay." I give him a smile and hand him a twenty-dollar bill.

I am looking in the mirror and hoping Meredith does not do anything to ruin the night. Just as I was about to walk out, Meredith walks in. Oh no.

"Well if it isn't Misses Popular." She says with such a dark laugh. I stand up. Take a deep breath. And mentally prepare myself for what comes next.

She grabs my hair and slams my head against the sink, then the mirror and it cracks, then she slaps me. She shoves me so hard I fall to the ground hitting my head. She kicks, stomps, punches, slaps and pulls me. She even rips my shirt.

She did not need Ariana nor Sophia. She could do more damage on her own. All of a sudden she stomps on my stomach so hard, I got the wind knocked out of me so hard I blacked out.

Asher's POV-

I just got off the phone with Mere and she said she wants to go to the movies and watch this new Horror film that came out called 'It' I think?

We met up there. As soon as Mere and I walk in I see Nate. Was he here alone? I look around and see Anastasia was beside him. Whoa, when the hell did this happen?

Anastasia looks around and sees me but as soon as she saw Mere the only thing that was evident on her face was fear. Was she scared of Meredith?

When we're right behind them, Anastasia asks Nate to buy her a ticket because she wanted to go to the restroom. "Ashy baby, can you do the same, I need to show Anastasia something." I nodded.

Something was off and but I, of course, did not care enough to wonder what it was.

A while has passed. Nate and I heard something break like glass in the bathroom but we let it be. Mere walks out with the biggest smirk. "Where is Ana?" Nate asks. Meredith smiles innocently and shrugs "Oh I don't know maybe she just wanted some space."

Nate gave her a death glare. He walks over to the girl's bathroom. "DUDE YOU AREN'T ACTUALLY GOING IN THERE, ARE YOU?" I yell out. I know he heard me but he doesn't reply.

He walks in and shouts "ANASTASIA!" Which made me want to go look at what happened. Nate keeps calling for help which caused people to go over there too.

I walked in. Complete shock was what I was in. Anastasia laid there, blood all around her, her shirt was ripped showing many bruises you couldn't even see her skin color. There was a piece of glass in her hair which caused me to look at the mirror.

Meredith slammed her into a mirror. God, she even ripped her shirt.

Since no one was doing anything besides Nate I tell him to call the hospital. I go in the middle of the crowd where she laid and picked her up.

I carried her to my car and Nate was following me while on the phone.

She was so light.

I speed down the road, passed red lights, didn't stop at stop signs. I may not care about Anastasia but god, she looked so much like my mom when she was laying there. She looked so...

lifeless.

We arrive at the hospital and the people put her on a bed and rolled her away. Nate and I sat in the waiting room.

"Why do you think Meredith did this?" I shrugged.

Why would she do this? Then time brought me back to the last time I saw her. The mall.

What I saw, the bruises on her face and neck, she was hiding them. She was the girl who was crying for Meredith to stop the day I showed up early for school.

It all adds up. Meredith hurts her and she never told anyone.

"She told me some sad shit, today man." Mumbled Nate His head was down.

I raised an eyebrow out of curiosity. "Her Dad and little brother, Ryder passed away last year in a car crash." I sat there in shock once again.

How did I not know about this? Does anyone know about this? Why did Anastasia hide this? Does her friend know about this?

As if Nate could read my mind "I don't think anyone knew man. I saw a dark purple spot around her eye and neck and thought my mind was fucking with me but they were actually bruises. And not once have I heard her dad and brother get in a car crash." I run my hands through my hair.

Nate is my best friend of 17 years. So he knows me and my thoughts pretty well at this point.

The more i thought about the more everything made sense. I stood up not saying a word. "Dude, where are you going?" Nate looked at me. I don't answer I just walk out the door and head to Meredith's house.

At Meredith's house

"MEREDITH MICKELSON GET THE HELL OUT HERE, NOW!" I yell slamming her door with the side of my fist.

The door unlocks showing Mere. "Why the hell did you do that Mere?" I said through gritted teeth. "Oh come on Asher you know you don't like her. You said you hated her even." I rolled my eyes.

"Well, why did you do it."

She looks to the ground with sad eyes then looks back up with cold ones and starts heading towards her door.

"She has everything that I want. A perfect family, a best friend who cares, god she even has so much attention and I don't know-how. So if hurting her makes me feel better, then I am going to keep doing it." She said growling. I now know Meredith has no idea what happened to Anastasia's Dad and little brother.

I also know she is a stone-cold bitch.

Going back to the hospital, I tell Nate everything that happened.

A couple of hours have passed and we both decided to come back tomorrow. I dropped Nate off because he used Anastasia's car.

Then I go home to mine. I go upstairs, everyone is sleeping. I throw my shirt off and fall on my bed. I don't care.

I don't care.

ch 7

Asher's POV-

I wake up on the floor with the memories of last night come flooding back. Quickly, I change, grab my keys, get a protein bar, then walk out the door.

First I drive to the cafe I saw Anastasia in, and order 2 chocolate muffins for Nate and Anastasia, Then head off to the hospital.

I see Nate already there. I walk over to him and give him the muffin. "Oh god, I love you, Asher Johnson." I laugh.

I saw Anastasia's mom walk in and I walk over to her. "Hi, I'm Asher." She got startled by my sudden introduction. "Ooh, gosh I'm so sorry, Hi I'm Anastasia's mom but you already knew that," she said with a slight laugh. Nate comes. "What happened last night Asher?" she asked.

Fuck I can't say its Meredith because I know no one wants their parents knowing this stuff. Nate and I shared a 'you tell her' look.

Nate is too scared so I had to.

"When we went to the movies last night she went to the restroom and random girls were hurting her." She looked down and tears filled her eyes.

"God, I knew she was hiding something" She gives us a weak smile.

"Anastasia Smith." a doctor called. All of our heads turn and walk up to her. "She is awake but if you guys talk to her, do it one at a time so it doesn't overwhelm her. She is in room 106." They nod and started walking there.

I tell Nate I'm leaving and to not tell Anastasia I was ever there.

With a nod, he walks to her room.

Anastasia's POV-

I woke up the nurse checking on me. "You have been damaged pretty bad Anastasia. I will give you pain meds because shit like this hurts." I chuckled at her words. What a good doctor right?

She gives me pain meds and water. I down the pill and she leaves.

I sit here just thinking. Almost laughing at myself for getting into this mess.

The door opens revealing my mom. "Mom?" "Oh sweetie, I'm so sorry about what those girls did to you. I will find them and report them. Are you okay? How are you doing? Why did you hide this from me? I knew something was going on. Oh dear, you look terrible. Why didn't you-"

"MOM?" she stops rambling. "I'm okay," I said reassuringly.

We had a long talk about what happened last night but it seems someone switched the story. I am not mad, I mean, I am thankful for whoever changed it.

After my mom is done she goes out. "Love you mom," I say before she walks out. "Love you, baby, I'll be back tomorrow."

Right, when she walks out Nate walks in. "Oh thank God you are okay!" He says being overdramatic. I giggle. "Thank you for making up a story." He looks at me "Uh, that wasn't me." I give him a 'wtf' look. He told me not to worry about it.

I open the bag to see a chocolate muffin. I smile.

Shit, I have to tell Violet what happened. She is probably flipping the hell out! I don't know where my phone is and i have a needle in my arm.

I decide to just wait until tomorrow.

The nurse walks in "I got your food. I know it's not good but you have to eat Anastasia." I nod. I got carrots, peas, water, and my eyes look at the last one in awe. Chocolate. Pudding. "I see you like chocolate pudding." She laughs. "I'll sneak you some more."

She winks then walks out. I have no idea who she is but I love her to death already.

Soon enough she walks in with 3 little cups of chocolate pudding.

"Thank you, thank you, thank you!" I smile wide and laugh.

She hands them over. "Okay now, mind to tell me how the hell you ended up in here? Don't worry everything you tell me is confidential so no one will know, not even your mom." I look at her nervously.

But, I explain everything. She is speechless. "Girl fight the bitch back. She is jealous of you if you can't already see that."

I laugh at how funny she sounds saying that in a doctor's outfit. "Okay back to serious business, anything else you want or need?"

My phone. I think to myself. "Is there any chance I can get my phone?" "Oh yes!" She gets my phone from my backpack. "Thank you?" I say trying to find her name tag. "Just call me Ashley." "Well, thank you, Ashley." I smile.

She walks out. When I go on my phone, I see that Violet spammed me with a lot of "where are you?" And "I am going to kill you next time I see you, Anastasia Ryan Smith."

V is scary as hell.

A long while passes by and the sun goes down. I got a room that was right in front of the sunset. I look at the sun until it goes down. It's stunning.

Now I lay here in this scary hotel room. I don't want to sleep so I go on Netflix and decide to watch Girls Trip.

I am laughing my ass off trying to stay quiet.

After the movie, I set my phone on the table next to me. Thank God Ashley put my things near me. I go to my backpack and pull out a book to read.

More time passes by and i check the time. 4 am. Sweet. I just keep reading.

I get so tired but I don't want to sleep at night in this scary hospital.

I put the book down and stare and lay down. I stare at the wall.

Ashley walks in "Hey I brought you some water and whoa I am guessing you didn't sleep?" "Do I look that bad?" I say. "Girl, you're beautiful but you look exhausted and need to sleep this bitch out."

Ashley is a dark woman with stunning long dark hair, she is talk and slim with curves in the right places. I envy her.

"Thank you, Ashley." She smiles. "Here." She says as she hands me the water. I was thirsty so i drank all of it. "You ready to eat?" I shake my head yes.

"Good because I spoke with your mom and she told me about this cafe and what your favorite thing to get is.

She hands me over a chocolate muffin with iced coffee. "You are my angel," I say. She laughs. "Hospital food is shitty so i figured you might like this.

"I love it."

Ashley sat down on the chair next to me. "I heard about your dad and brother, Ryder is it?" I nod. "I am so sorry girl. That shit is hectic as hell but God has his reasons baby." I nod again.

Tears in my eyes "Yeah, I guess so."

We talk about some cool things like how she used to be the captain of her cheerleading team in high school. She sings and plays the piano. She loves writing and adores drawing. She is a single mom with a baby girl.

Ashley is one powerful woman.

"Awe man time to go see my other patient." I smile and wave bye.

She peeps her head through the door. "Oh, by the way, you might be able to be free today from this cage we call a hospital." I laugh and pump my fist in the air overdramatically "Yes." I say.

She leaves with a laugh. I drink my coffee and eat my chocolate muffin. I look at my phone time. Holy hell it's already 7:30 in the morning? I get my book out and start reading. I set my coffee on the side table.

My mom walks in. "Hey, mom." "Hey sweetie, you are able to leave today!" "Oh thank God, i hate this place."

"Let me get the doctor to get you out."

Soon enough the doctors walk in, checks me then let me go. My mom is talking to the desk lady. Ashley walks up to me and sits beside me. "Leaving so soon?" "Yeah, I am." "Well here, my number in case you need anything."

Even though she was my doctor I trust her. I take the little folded up piece of paper and put it in my pocket.

She leaves. "Ready?" My mom asks. I nod. And we head to her car.

We go home. "You won't be going to school for a bit okay?" "Yeah, thank you."

I go to my room and take off my clothes only leaving on my bra and panties. I look at myself in the body mirror i have in the corner of my room. Wow, I look so bad.

I get out of the rest of my undergarments then hop in the shower. This was very much needed.

***

I have been in been watching TV all day and my mom has babied me nonstop. My eyes wander around my room. I see the old shoebox that I stuffed old pictures in. I limp my way over to the closet and try and reach the top. I can't.

After a while of trying I completely gave up. I was so tired and so sore, I had not one ounce of energy left in me to just make my way over to my bed. So I lay on the floor and fall asleep.

Sorry, there are so many mistakes!!! I'll fix them but I need to post a chapter.

ch 8

✱ ** 2 weeks later ***

    I haven't talked to anyone besides Violet for the past 2 FREAKING WEEKS.

I am almost fully healed and the bruises are all gone. It is still painful doing things like stretching and running but hey, I'm getting there.

School is tomorrow and since I look presentable again, I can go! Never thought I'd say this but. I actually missed going to school.

I know, shocker right?

I am at home, alone. My body is wrapped in a towel along with my hair. I am sitting on my bed with a face mask on.

All I did most of the 2 weeks was to stay home alone and draw. So not fun.

I only went out once and that was just another check-up at the doctor's.

It's about 5 in the evening and I am waiting for my mom to get off work.

She owns 5 businesses so she is always running around the town. One of her buildings is in New York City. Lucky.

I definitely look up to that woman.

Anyways, I am now looking for pajamas along with clothes for school tomorrow. I don't know why but I feel like I should really show up looking good to show Meredith off.

I am not letting her mess around with me anymore. Putting my mom and Violet through that is never going to happen again.

I change into a big t-shirt and spandex.

As I was combing my hair, I heard something outside of my window and my head darts up.

I always have the knife, my dad gave me when I turn 15. I take it out of my nightstand drawer.

I peek outside the window and see someone standing out there with their hands in their hoodie and the hoodie on their heads.

Oh hell no. Not today.

I hide behind my curtain as I keep looking through the window so the person won't see me. They start walking towards the front door. FUCK.

Then I hear knocking on my front door. I look up and close my eyes "Jesus, I don't want to die today so if you love me, you won't let that happen." I practically begged.

I slowly walk downstairs. It's dark, the only light on was my bedroom light. I grab my phone in my hand and turn on the flashlight.

I am in front of the door.

I silently do a prayer. I look through the peephole and I am beyond shocked to see who it was.

I unlock it slowly and there he is.

"Asher?"

He laughs. "Seriously Anastasia? You thought I was a killer or something?"

"Who wouldn't think that? Look at you, your hands are in your pocket, hoodie on and it's black. So do not ask that because yes I thought you were."

I said keeping in a laugh because I know I looked stupid holding a knife.

He looks at me and observes me. I don't mind this time, it's dark out and he can't see anything. I observe him too. The street light is lighting his eyes up.

A few moments later. "Oh, come in, it's freezing," I say opening the door more.

"Want anything to drink or eat?" He nods his head no. I go into my kitchen and turn on the lights.

He sits on the island stool. I put my hair up in a messy bun and take the front pieces out. "Well, I am making hot chocolate and you are having it whether you like it or not." He nodded and chuckled.

After the making of the hot cocoa, I pour them into mugs and sit in front of him on the other side of the island.

Moments passed and no one has said anything. He looks like he is thinking about something that makes it look like he is getting angrier each minute.

1, 2, 3, 4, 5 almost 6 minutes pass.

He slowly brings his gaze to me. He blinks 3 times. "Are you okay?" I ask concerned.

"I should be asking you that." I hum.

"Well, I am okay. Are you?" He doesn't answer. I take a sip of my hot chocolate. "So, um," I say trying to think of what to say. "How was your day?"

Seriously Ana? Are you stupid? "How was your day?" Really?

I mentally slap myself in the face. "It was like every other day." I nodded and looked down fidgeting with my fingers. I'm nervous.

My phone rings. Mom? "I'm sorry," I say and he just nods. I walk into the living room.

"Mom, hey what's up?"

"Hey sweetie, I am going to be out for a few days. I met this guy and he is really sweet Ana, I think we might be hitting it off."

Is she fucking serious right now? What about dad? Ryder even. Did she forget about that?

I tear up. Keeping myself from breaking down.

"Okay, well just remember Dad and Ryder while you have the time of your life with other men," I say with my voice cracking.

"Wait Ana I know you might not agree with-"

I hung up and threw my phone. It is broken.

Taking a deep breath I tell myself "just smile till the nights over Ana."

I smile and turn around about to make my way to the living room. I stop.

I could feel my heart fall out of my ass when I saw Asher standing at the entrance of the living room. I flop on the couch.

He saw everything.

I put my face in my hands and try my best not to cry. I felt the couch get lower so I know Asher sat down next to me. "I'm sorry," I say.

"Why are you sorry?" He asks. "I don't really know." He shrugs and leans back.

"Why are you here Asher?" I ask.

He looks at me with a blank face. "I just wanted to see if you healed. Looks like you have so I will leave now." He says.

"Also don't tell anyone I was here." He says coldly and harsh.

It was almost terrifying hearing him say how he did. So slow and calm but deadly almost. Like he had just flipped a switch that turned off his feelings and emotions.

I all of a sudden feared Asher Johnson.

My eyes only head fear. His face went held a different emotion for just a second then back to emotionless. He then walked out and slammed the door.

My stomach is turning. Next thing you know I am on my hands and knees throwing all of what is inside of me up. I got so dizzy.

Asher storms in "I forgot my phone." He said through gritted teeth.

He headed towards the kitchen. He didn't see me thank God.

"Holy shit." He says. He runs to me and kneels down rubbing my back and holding my hair. "No no no please go away."

He doesn't listen.

I get up and go to my bathroom. He follows me. I almost fall over but I held onto the table for more support.

I spit in the toilet then take an extra toothbrush from the drawer and brush my teeth. When I am done I throw it away because ew. I put both hands on my counter. I take a deep breath.

You're okay Ana. It's okay. Everything is okay. I mentally say.

I try walking but I keep half falling. "Jesus Christ," Asher says.

He carries me and at this point, I am so weak I can't even carry myself up and keep my eyes open.

He walks up the stairs. "Which is your room." I barely point to my door. He opens it and lays me down in my bed. My eyes are closed but I can feel him putting my blankets over me.

After that, my mind went blank.

So Asher isn't THAT bad?

ch 9

The following day Anastasia went to the doctors again to see what was wrong with her the night before. Ashley said it was probably something she ate.

2 days have passed and finally Anastasia decided it was time for school, she has missed so much already she knew she couldn't skip any more days.

Sadly, her mind can't remember what happened with Asher.

(ANASTASIA'S POV)

It is only 4 in the morning and I haven't been able to sleep. School starts in 4 hours.

Might as well just get ready.

I go downstairs to make breakfast first.

Of course, cereal.

Morning showers are the best showers so I take one. I shave, exfoliate, wash my face, and brush my teeth all in one shower. Now it's 6:30 am.

I throw on my outfit and apply some makeup. Since I have so much time, I decide to apply just a tad bit more makeup on.

(H E R F I T)

Time passed and since I still have a bit more time, I go to the river.

****

Now I'm on the rock and have been drawing. its 7 am so I have to start going soon. I put my things inside my bag then head to my car.

When I am in my car I get nervous to go to school. 3 weeks.

3 whole weeks since I have been in that building. I hope no one knows what happened. Only the teachers know. But no one besides the people who were there knows it was Meredith.

I pull up at the school. I see Asher and Nate with there group. "Please make everything be normal," I said with my fingers crossed.

By normal I mean, no encounters with Asher. I get out of my car.

So many eyes were on me. I was nervous but I refuse to let that show. I take a deep breath and walk.

"Hey Anastasia""Ana, nice fit.""Hey, An!"

I got greets from people. So far so good.

I walk past Asher's group a little faster. I could feel them all staring. "Ana, hey!" I knew it was Nate so I turn around slowly.

I see him and do an awkward wave. He walks up to me and says bye to his friends.

We are now walking to class. I never knew he was in most of my classes. We head to 1st period together.

"How are you?" He asks. "I am fine, just a bit weird coming back after 3 whole weeks." A laugh escapes him. "Makes sense, don't worry, from the looks of it, almost everyone here loves you." I smile.

"ANASTASIA RYANA FUCKING SMITH!" Oh no. I slowly turn around. "Hiiii Violetttt," I said dragging out the words.

She walks up to me and pushes me. Shocked, "What the fuck was that for?" I said almost pissed off by that. "You had me worrying for 3 whole weeks Anastasia. And I am sorry for pushing you, that wasn't right."

I hug her. "I was just super sick, I'm sorry for not calling." She nodded and walked to class with me and Nate. "Are y'all a thing?" She asks.

Nate and I looked at each other. We just shook our heads no.

****

The day passed and it's lunchtime now. Me and Nate, Violet, and I decided to get pizza. We all took my car.

"No, you blonde boy. I want the front."

"No, I called it already!"

I just sit in the driver's seat laughing. Eventually, they decided Violet can get the front on the way there and Nate gets the front on the way back.

We pull up at the pizza place and take out seats. We are in a booth. Nate is next to me and V is in front of us.

"Girl you look bomb as hell today." I smile at V's comment.

A girl came to us and took our orders. She eyed Nate and was flirting with him. She turned around and swayed her hips.

"Dude she is totally into you."

He looks at me and shakes his head no. "I don't like those types of girls." I shrug.

She comes back with the pineapple pizza we ordered. "Be right back."

I get up to pay so they don't tell me no. Then I use the restroom. I take my phone out and snap a quick selfie. "Not bad," I say to myself.

I go out and go back to Nate and V.

It has been nothing but stupid jokes and laughs. Nate is a cool guy. I noticed him and V was eyeing each other. I smirk.

"Guys I am going to go back I forgot my phone." I walk up and get out.

V is so going to beat my ass.

***

I am at school. I sit under the tree and pull out my book from my bag.

I feel a pair of eyes on me. I slowly look up and look around.

Asher is looking at me. I close my book, put it near my chest, get my bag, then go to my car. There are still 45 minutes left of lunch. I guess I will just stay in my car.

My eyes wander around the people. They all seem so happy with life.

My attention is suddenly on Asher. He is still looking at me. I take a deep breath and place my head on the steering wheel.

My mind travels back to the night of the movies. I start crying. The more I think about it, the angrier and sad I feel. I punch the steering wheel.

Which was a mistake, my hand hurts.

I am sobbing at this point.

After about 5 minutes. I take a deep breath and fix my makeup. When I'm done I put the car in drive. I give a glance at Asher. He is still looking.

I stop the car and get out. In front of the car door, I stand looking back at him. He is pissing me off.

He starts walking over to me angrily. "shit" I mumble.

He pushes me against my car. "What the fuck is your problem." He growls. I shove him off of me considering he was so close. "Your eyes are glued on me, is something wrong with me?" I say pissed off. "Yes actually, everything about you is wrong."

I was a bit taken back. I stare at him in disbelief. Next thing I know, tears start forming. "Wait I'm-"

"Shut the fuck up and leave me the hell alone." I cut him off before he could say anything. I go in my car and drive away.

I pull up at the pizza place. I see Nate and V smiling and laughing. I walk over to them. "Hey, guys! You ready to go?"

They nod. "Ana, I thought you just needed your phone?" V asks. I shrug.

The whole car ride back V and Nate were talking like there was no tomorrow. I stayed quiet.

We arrive at school and head to the next class. "You are lucky you get to leave after this," V says. I half-smile.

"Are you okay, you are a bit off right now."

"Yeah Ana, you good?"

They both ask. I nod and smile reassuringly. They believe me.

We all head to class.

The class was crap. Asher and Nate were talking. Violet was talking to Nate.

I kept my head down most of the time. The only time it went up was when I had to write things down.

I am heading to my car. I see Asher and he sees me, rolling his eyes, he scoffs and puts a cancer stick in his mouth.

With that, I walk into my car and go home.

"MOM?" I call out. Seriously mom? You should be here. I think to myself.

I head up to my bedroom and do school work. I skipped dinner and just watched tv. I eventually fell asleep.

*********Author's note

hey guys! there are mistakes, I know. I will edit it soon! hope you like this chapter:)

ch 10

(ANASTASIA'S POV)

I wake up to another 'no mom'.

Today is Thursday which means the party is tomorrow and everyone will be talking about it today.

Today school ends early, thank god.

I do my everyday morning routine then head out the door.

(her fit)

On the drive there I stop by Petite Cafe, of course. I get 2 iced coffees and 2 chocolate muffins. I saw Nate with Violet. HOLY SHIT!

I plaster the biggest grin on my face and walk over to them. They look at me and turn red. "You guys are so cute!" I say slightly jumping.

"You hooked us up Ana, Violet is very much exquisite." He says. Violet turns into a cherry. I wink then walk into my car.

Awe man, I got 2 of each of the things I got.

One of both for V but she is already getting something. Who am I supposed to give these to?

I put the cups in the cup holders and the white bag with the muffins in the passenger seat.

When I pull up there is a crowd around 2 people. "What the hell?" I walk out and see almost everyone look at me. I take a sip of my coffee and walk to them.

As I am trying to push people away so I can see. I catch a glimpse of Asher and this other guy fighting.

Asher is literally going to kill him and no one is doing anything. I go to tell him to stop then-

All of a sudden someone grabs me. "Hey, sorry but if you went into that crazy fight, you would have gotten really hurt." I look up. It was a girl I have never seen before.

She had long blonde hair, bright blue eyes, perfect lips, and a flawless body.

"Are you new? I have never seen you before?" She shook her head up and down. "Do you want a chocolate muffin and iced coffee?" She looks at me questioning. "I was supposed to give it to my best friend Violet but I couldn't.

Don't worry, i didn't put anything bad inside of them." She smiles "Yeah sure."

We head to my car and I give them to her. She is actually super cool and enjoys the same things as me. "Wanna go sit somewhere?" I ask. She smiled and nodded.

We sat under the tree I always sit at. "So what brings you to this odd town?" "My dad got a job in this town. He said he couldn't stand working in the town where my mom left us. And we thought a change would be nice."

"I'm sorry," I say. "also, consider me your first friend also," I said with a wink.

She laughed. "I never got your name?" I ask. "Its Loren."

I see Violet and her boy toy Nate pull up. "Let me introduce you to my best friend and her boyfriend." She laughs.

V and Nate see us walk towards us. "Hey guys, this is Loren and she is new." She waves, obviously a bit shy. "Hey, girl! I'm Violet and this is Nate." She smiles at Loren. "Hi, I'm Nate." They shake hands.

V and Nate went to class but right now I am going to the office with Loren to get her schedule.

"Name." The office ladies here are kind of mean but I don't blame them, the kids here are disrespectful. "Loren O'neil."

The woman takes a piece of paper out of her file box and hands it to Loren. With nothing else said, we walk out.

"Our schedules are almost identical! Let's go to 1st." I walk and she follows.

When I open the door I bring her to the teacher so they can talk about the things she missed and so on. I see V and Nate together flirting. Oh god. I sit in the back today because I wanted to finish one of my drawings, plus this class is beyond easy. No Asher today. Kowijg him, he was probably in the office.

I go and take a seat. "Jake can you move so Loren can sit next to Ana please." The guy moves and Loren sits.

The rest of the class was me and Loren talking while I show her some of my drawings. She seems very fascinated with my art.

As the classes went on I got even more tired but now we are walking to lunch. I'm more and I are going to Petite Cafe while V and Nate go I don't even know where.

"You are very pretty," Loren says out of nowhere. I just smile at her comment. "Can I um, have the aux." I nod and let her.

She turns on Fool For You by Zayn. Which is one of my favorite songs?

Cause I'm a fool for youAnd the things you doI'm a fool for youAnd the things, the things you doThe things you doThe things you do

We are singing our lungs out to this song and it turns out she can actually sing.

We arrive at the cafe. I get my usual and she just gets water with an oatmeal cookie.

We take the seat near the big window. Of course.

We go on and on about random things like music and school and boys. She is very easy to talk to.

Time passes and we head back to the school and head to our next period. I leave after this thank God.

The teacher is a bit grumpy. No one in the world is surprised. More and more people walk in and take their seats. "Just take the worksheet of the desk and work on it till class is over." Everyone obeys with grabbing the sheets but no one obeys actually doing it.

Violet, Nate, and Loren are talking while I space out. I decide to do the worksheet and leave early.

I hand it up. "May I leave please." She shoos me off. I wave the other bye.

Instead of going to my car I sit under a tree. I get out a book and just read.

"What are you doing." I hear someone say with no emotion.

I look up to see a beaten up Asher. So that's why he wasn't in this period. I think to myself.

I take a small first aid kit out of my bad and motion him to sit down. He seemed a bit weak so he sits.

I take a small wipe and wipe off the blood around his face and arms. "What happened to you?" I ask.

"Why do you care." I take a deep breath and don't say anything else.

Why do you have to be so fucking rude? I did nothing. In fact, I'm helping you. I wanted to say so bad.

"Just get some rest and don't move around so much maybe?" I get up and walk towards my car.

As I was about to get into my car I feel someone tug on my arm. I turn around to see once again, Asher.

"Thank you." He says sternly then walks away. I start there dumbfounded.

*****

After that, I went straight home and kept reading my book.

Now, I am cooking dinner for myself. I burnt my wrist on accident. I laugh at myself.

When I'm done I sit on the chair in front of the island. I call my mom.

Me- Mom when are you coming home?

Mom- I don't know yet honesty, I'm having f-fun!

Me - Mom are you drunk?

Mom- Shhhh

Me- Mom, where are you?

Mom- S-secrett

She hangs up.

I keep calling her and calling her. She won't answer.

I throw my phone and run my fingers through my hair.

I go change into grey sweats and a white hoodie, get into my car and drive.

I see a bridge and a parking area. The sun is about to set.

I park then sit on top of my car. I cuddle my knees into my stomach. It's cold but I don't want to be at home.

The sunset is so calming. I hop down and get my drawing book and pencils.

I draw the sun and the trees aligning the bridge.

Before I knew it, it was dark out. I lie down. And stare up. Cars passed by and probably looked me crazily but I didn't mind.

That is until a car parked a few spots away from me.

A guy steps out of his Lambo and lies on top of it. He is wearing gray sweats and a white hoodie. I quietly laugh.

We were wearing literally the same thing.

I sit up and stare off into the distance. I felt the guy looking at me. I slowly took in his direction.

I gasp and take a closer look.

Asher?

I give him a small smile and a wave. He gets off of his car and gets in.

I frown thinking he is going to drive off but instead,

he leaves the spot he was parked in and parks in the spot right next to me.

He then gets out and sits back on top of his car.

We laid on our backs look at the stars in silence.

****

I hope u guys are enjoying the book!

ch 11

Asher's POV-

It is around 5 in the morning and I have been up all night reading.

I don't believe in the love that exists in the books but I like to imagine.

Silently, I put the book down and turn on the tv. I scroll through Netflix and see nothing good then shut the tv off. I sigh and look around for something to do.

Nothing.

I groan and get up. Might as well just just leave.

I throw on a decent outfit, do my hair, brush my teeth, then splash cold water on my face.

By the time I'm done, it's 6:56. What the hell? Since when did I take this long to get ready? I go wake up Abigail and make breakfast for her.

French toast and eggs, her favorite.

I hear her tiny footsteps walk downstairs. She was in a white t-shirt, light washed overalls, and her small white converse. I smile at her. "Well don't you look nice today, who is the boy?" She laughs. "ew boys have cooties, yucky."

I hand the plate over to her and she chows down on it. When she is done we get in the car and of course, she screams along with the loud engine.

We head to a gas station and I buy her some snacks for the day. "Thank you ashy." She smiles.

Then I dropped her off at her school.

***

I am now at school and I'm with my friends. Nate isn't here and I heard him and Violet are hitting it off.

Nate is more of the good guy in the group, he never fucks around with girls, never smokes, but he drinks occasionally.

I, on the other hand, does everything he doesn't. I drink, smoke, party, always get in fights and fuck around with girls.

Typical.

There are 6 people in the group. Nate, Josh, Daniel, Zach, Jonah and me, Asher.

Everyone is talking about the stupid party tomorrow that I have no intention of going to.

"Anastasia is hot as fuck, I'd fuck her," Zach says. I shake my head in disgust with how they talk about girls. "Oh c'mon Ash, you have to agree. She is the hottest girl in our school."

I roll my eyes and look away. "I'm spiking her drink at the part tomorrow." He says.

I grab him by the collar. "No. No, you fucking won't." I growl. He just laughs. "If you want to do it, man, then okay, she is all yours. I'll find another girl." I feel my blood start to boil.

I punch him in the eye. That ticked him off. One punch after another.

2 minutes go by and the fight is still going on. More and more people kept crowding. I could have sworn I saw Anastasia too.

*****

The great of the day goes by and I'm skipping class. Most people have a free period but mine is more towards the end of the day.

I was walking behind the school to look at the view.

Riverbank High was right next to a river. Many trees and flowers surrounded the place.

The river was in my sight till I got pulled in the opposite direction. I felt the body hit the ground and see Zach and a few more lowlifes surrounding me. I scoff.

"You really think beating the shit out of me will do anything? Yeah okay." He gives me a wicked grin.

He puts to fingers in the air and signals the rest to 'go' after me.

I am on the cement with about 3 to 4 guys on me. I'm used to this shit, it doesn't bother me. I just wait till they are done hitting me.

When they are done I struggle to get up but I do. I head back inside to clean myself up. For a free period, no one was around.

I see a girl reading I think. I head towards her. I shook my head seeing who it was.

Anastasia?

"What are you doing?" I say sternly. She looks at me and her eyes are big for a second. She proceeds to think.

She is digging in her backpack for something. I see a first aid kit in her hand. Who the hell just carries those around.

Her hands motioned me to sit. I think for a split second then obey. Using a small wipe, she wipes the blood off.

"What happened to you?" She seemed worried. "Why do you care?" I say rudely. She takes a deep breath which makes me know she is trying to notsap back at me.

It's funny.

She tells me stuff like 'rest' and 'don't move so much' She then gets her things and walks away. I run my fingers through my hair.

I get up and jog to her. Before she opened her car I tugged on her arm and say, "Thank you." She looks shocked.

But saying nothing else, I walk in the other direction.

*****

School is over and I'm in my bed with Abigail. It's around 11 pm. Abi is sleeping and I can't even shut my eyes.

What Zach said today pissed me off. It's one thing saying she is hot, but physically saying you would spike her drink?

Thinking about it makes me want to punch something. Instead of doing that I ball up my fists for a moment because Abi is in my arms. I slowly get up and place her on the bed, tuck her in, then kiss her on the forehead.

I put a white sweatshirt with grey sweats on. I put my Nike air force 1's on, get my keys then head out the door.

When I arrive at my location I see a girl there on her car. I chuckle seeing we are wearing the same thing. She is looking at me.

I hop out of my car and sit on top of it. The feeling that her eyes are on me is gone, so, I take that as a chance to look in her direction. Anastasia? Why the hell would she be here so late?

She slowly looks in my direction.

I can hear her gasp when she realizes it's me. She gives me a small smile along with one of her cheezy waves.

How can someone be so cheery?

I get down and get in my car. I was about to drive away when I see her frowning. She probably thinks I despise her. Her frown made me change my mind about leaving. I take a deep breath. "Fuck it," I say.

I drive to where she is and park my car in the parking space right beside her. I get back in my car. I see her small smile. I smile too but she doesn't see that.

She lies down on her back and looks up at the bright lights the sky is providing. I do the same.

We just lie there. Nothing said, no one interacting. Just laying there. Weird thing is, it's not awkward. The silence is comfortable. She gives off a good aura.

She stays for about an hour then leaves. It's 1 in the morning and I head home too. Before I do I saw a notebook in her parking spot. I pick it up and on the front says, Anastasia Smith. I put it inside my car and head home.

I crawl in bed and see Abi is still there. I scoot her over so she doesn't take up all the room. Then I lay down and drift off.

―――――

Authors Note

I hope y'all enjoyed this chap!! :)

ch 12

Don't forget to vote!

It is lunch and so far today no one has talked about anything but the party, which by the way, I don't even want to go to but I promised Violet I would go.

Right now I am sitting at a lunch table with Violet, Nate, Asher, and the group of his friends. My elbow is on the table holding my head up because of how tired I am.

I'm picking at the mash potatoes with my spoon.

I get up and walk away. I am bored and want to read so I do so.

I go behind the school and sit on the grass with my back on a beautiful tree with white flowers. Realizing I forgot my book on the lunch table, I just sit there and take in the view.

Flowers and big trees surround the area, the water is flowing so smoothly and the small waterfall is the best part.

I get up and sit under another tree with white flowers but it's right in front of the water.

I put my hand in the water and play with it. I see Asher sit on another side of the tree. "Why did you leave the table?" He asks in his normal no emotion voice. "I was bored and wanted to read out here but.. I forgot my book at the lunch table." I say with a frown.

He holds up my book and says, "this one?" I nod my head happily and I try and grab it. He moved his hand so I couldn't. "Oh no, you didn't." He smirked.

So now I am chasing Asher trying to get my book but-

1, he is tall

2, a fast ass runner

3. impossible to catch

So I fall down dramatically and say, "I'm out of breath Asher, let me breathe." He laughs and falls down next to me.

I take a glance at him.

You aren't so bad.

I think to myself. I smile.

'Wait here.' he says.

Soon enough he is back with a different book in his hand.

My heart fell right out of my ass.

It was my drawing book.

'Don't worry, I didn't look through it.' I let out the biggest sigh.

'Would you like to?' He looks at me with questioned face. 'Yeah.' he said with a shrug. I hand it to him and we leave.

We both walk in the school and eyes are glued onto us.

I think Asher realized I was uncomfortable when he said: "Stop staring." Loud enough for everyone to hear.

With that, no more eyes we're on us. My jaw about hit the floor when he got everyone to do that. He looks at me and laughs.

The mean and ruthless Asher that I know is a different person when he laughs.

We both head to class. "Don't you get to leave after this class?" I nod my head yeah. "Well, you are lucky as hell." He says pouting.

I almost died of laughter when a tough guy like him pouted.

When we walk in, everybody is to busy talking to notice us. The teacher is sleeping. We head to our normal seats.

"Hey!" Violet and Loren say in unison. I wave. "Loren where we're you at lunch?" I ask. "Oh, I went to my house to eat." I smile and nod.

Of course, the class was boring. Me and Asher exchange glances. All of a sudden I get a text.

Unknown- it's not over.

Me- who is this

Unknown- oh you know me. stay away from Asher or so God help me i will ruin you and hurt your drunk mom.

I gulp and look around. I feel the color drain from my face. I think Asher noticed when he gave me a raised eyebrow.

Gathering my things, I run out. I start breathing heavily and my hand his over my chest.

I am having a panic attack.

I see Asher come out of the classroom and when he sees me, he runs over to me. He sits me down on the floor and holds me, slowly stroking his fingers through my hair which calmed me down.

My dad did the same thing when I had my first break up.

Asher motioned me to follow him to his car.

So I did.

*****

An amusement park. A fricking amusement park is where he brought me!

There he was just standing with a straight face while I was looking around.

My eyes glow.

Cotton candy.

Asher looks at what I am looking at. "You get pumped up over cotton candy?' It may sound stupid but cotton candy is MY addiction. We head over there.

That is until I bump into someone and land right on my ass.

"Watch it ugly ass." I felt a hole in my stomach. I get up and see that it's a tall muscular man with tattoos, how intimidating.

"I'm so sorry, I- I didn't mean to bump into you," I say with fear clear in my voice. He smirks and comes closer.

Asher shows up out of nowhere, literally, and punches the guy, provoking him.

The guy tries to punch back but Asher beats him. Asher keeps going in going.

I go up to him and gently grab his arm and pull him away.

"Asher, Asher, look at me. See? I'm okay, everything is okay." I smile nervously.

He looks at the guy and stands up. "Don't. Fucking. Touch. Her." The guy smirks. "She is a freak anyway." Asher kicks him so hard in the face, he gets knocked out.

I look up and realize people we're watching. I felt sick. Asher begins walking away with his fists in a ball with gritted teeth.

I run up to him. I grab his arm and turn him around. "Hey, hey, it's okay, I promise, let's just go. Okay?" He nods.

We walk back to his car. We just sit there. "Thank you," I say.

He doesn't say anything but put the car in drive.

****

We arrive at my house and he drops me off. "Keep the notebook by the way."

"Are you sure?" I smile and nod. "Thank you for a good day, I needed one," I say. "Well, that makes 2 of us."

****

Violet and Loren are at my house getting ready. Its 6:14 pm on the dot and the party starts at 8.

I throw on the outfit I bought the day my mom and Ashers mom made an encounter.

It was this stunning red dress paired with a light washed oversized denim jacket. Shoes didn't come with it sadly so i put black heels on.

I look at myself in the mirror and snap a pic. The dress hugged my body nicely and the denim jacket gives it more flair. I put my hair up in a bun leaving pieces of hair out.

I walk out and do my makeup. I went a little bold, but since it was probably the first and last party I am going to junior year, might as well go all out, am I right?

Once I am satisfied with my look I smile. Not bad Smith. I say to myself.

I make sure the denim jacket hangs off my shoulders, then I head downstairs to the guest room where Loren and V are.

"Holy hell you look, HOT ," V says. "Anastasia, you look perfect what the hell, how?" I smile and Loren's comment.

Violet is wearing black and Loren is wearing Gold. Suits them.

V checks the time, "7:56" she says. "Fashionably late?" She asks.

"Fashionably late," I say.

Going late is me and V's thing when we go to parties together.

"You both look stunning." They smile.

We go to my car and go to the Petite Cafe. They get cookies and I didn't get anything. I was too nervous to eat.

I have no intention of getting drunk so I am just going to drink water tonight.

***

We pulled up to the party and loud music is blaring through the neighborhood while red cups are all over the front lawn. I see couples making out and drunk boys being drunk boys.

This is going to be one hell of a night.

———————————

AUTHORS NOTE

Enjoy:)

Make sure to vote!

ch 13

Violet, Loren, and I walk in and receive many stares and whistles.

Not happening.

The music is blaring and people are dancing. Violet walked off somewhere, Loren and I are waiting for her in the big crowd of hormonal teenagers.

She comes back with 3 shots. Oh no. No drinking Ana, c'mon. "V I am not drinking," I say. "Oh come on Ana, loosen up a bit!" She yells.

The music is so loud I can barely hear her.

"I'm the one driving you guys V. I am staying sober." She gives up and nods. They down the shots. Loren is looking off into the distance and I slowly turn around to see who it is. Meredith? Why would she be looking at Meredith? But I didn't realize Meredith was starting at us. Hm.

"Let's dance!" Loren and Violet said in unison. I nod and they both get a grip on my hands while pulling me to the dance floor.

**

We have been dancing for God who knows how long. All 3 of us are against each other swaying our hips to the music.

Time passes and Nate showed up and took Violet. Loren and I are dancing with each other and the boys are looking at us and whistling. We both agreed to not let boys fuck up our fun.

We were all sweaty and a messy so we go to the restroom to freshen ourselves up. When we walk to the restroom I see Nate and V sitting on the bar stools talking. Awe.

**

I look at myself in the mirror and to be honest, I don't look that bad, but, I added more spice taking my hair down and letting it flow. I then touch up my makeup. Loren did the same. "We look hot girl." I laugh.

**

We decide to take a small break from the party and sit on the couch. Next to us are 2 girls making out and on the other side, there are drunk kids acting foolish. But its a party so fuck it I guess.

***Loren and I were talking nonsense for about 15 minutes.

I had an uneasy feeling like someone was staring at me. I look around the room and see Meredith giving me a glare that sent shivers down my spine. I suck it up and smirk.

Getting up, I go to one of the random boys on the dance floor and dance.

She is starting so I might as well put on a show for her.

**

Loren went off with this guy Zach I think it is his name so now I am on the couch by myself.

That same uneasy feeling came back so I again scan the room to see Meredith starting at me. This girl is really a freak.

I decide to just take 1 drink to loosen up just a tad bit. It helped for sure. I look around the room to see if there are any places with fewer people. As I was searching I bump into someone.

"I am so sorry I didn't see you!" I say quickly. "What is up with you and bumping into people?" My head darts up with the sound of the voice. "Oh Asher, " I say with my hand over my chest "it's just you."

"Where are you going?" He asks. "Well my friends are with guys and I am alone so I wanted to find a free space to hang out for a while." He then motioned me to follow him.

We arrive in the backyard of the house. There was a pool, hammock, and an outdoor seating area. Wow, rich much?

He motions for me to sit down, I do, then he sits next to me making sure there is the distance between us.

I lean back on the soft sofa and look up at the star-filled sky. 1..2..3 deep breaths. "You came," I said. "Yeah, I guess I was bored." I don't say anything.

Minutes pass by then I think, does he know who Zach is?

"Hey, I have a question." He looks at me expectantly. "Do you know who Zach?" His face turned cold, emotionless almost. "Yes, why?" He growled.

"Umm..my friend Loren went with him and I don't know who he is." He looks at me wide-eyed.

Grabing me, starts running back inside. He said something under his breath like don't hurt her.

His hand still on my wrist, he rushes upstairs. There are about 8 rooms in this house and he managed to kick down the door to each of them. "What is going on?" I say worried. "He had a plan of spiking girls drink.

It was going to be you but I said no and he didn't like it so I fought him. Now he is going for someone else."

I look at him with teary eyes. God Loren, please be okay.

"NO STOP."

We heard a scream and ran to it. We went to the room and tried to open the door.

It was locked. Asher kicked down the door and there she was, on the bed, clothes off except her bra and underwear with Zach trying to take them off.

Asher runs to him and pushes him off. "Oh come on man, you ruined my fun."

Asher is getting fumed up and you can see it on his face he wanted to kill him. "You're sick." He says the gritted teeth pointing at each who is on the floor.

I run over to Loren and she is devastated. I hold her, her body is shaking and she is crying uncontrollably.

"It's okay, it's okay. I'm here." I run my fingers through her hair and try to calm her down.

Asher is fighting Zach. Punch after punch Zach gets weaker. With how Asher is hitting, it looks like he has been waiting to do this for a while.

I grab Loren's clothes and help her put them on. Zach is on the floor knocked out. He looks at Loren, then me, then back at Loren. His face went soft just for a split second, then back to stone cold. He walks out of the room.

I have Loren leaning ln my shoulder while we try to find V. I see her.

"Oh my God. What the hell happened?" V looks at Loren and me in shock.

After explaining everything, she leaves with us.

**

Right now she is comforting Loren in the backseat while I speed to my house.

**

We arrive. I open the front door and my mom is on the couch. "Good God, what the hell happened?!" I explain everything to my mom.

She doesn't call Loren's parents, but she helps us take care of her. My mom believes that this is Loren's story, not hers to tell.

**

Loren is asleep in my guest room. I already texted her mom pretending to be her saying she was "staying at a friend's house."

V and I are on the couch drinking tea. "God, I pray she will be okay soon. She almost witnessed the rape, and Zach spiked her drink."

When she puts it into words I feel a big pit in my stomach. I get up and change into warm and comfy clothes, get my keys and head out the door. "Where are you going?" V asks. "I need to clear my head."

She nods and I go.

***

I am at the bridge again. It's really late but I need to put my mind at ease.

After about an hour, the same black Lamborghini parks beside me. Asher is here.

"Hey," I say while he is getting in his car. "Hey."

Moments of silence pass by, comfortable silence.

The more I think of what happened the sicker I feel. I put my hands in my hair. Tears start to fall.

I hide my face in my sweatshirt hood. "I know you're crying, you don't need to hide it." I slowly take my hood off and take a deep breath.

"It's hard," I say. He gets off of his car and climbed up to mine and puts his arm around me while stroking my hair. "I know." He says softly.

I stayed there crying for a while.

**

It was 3 in the morning and I figured maybe it's time to go home. "Thank you," I say quietly. He nods. "Are you going home yet?" I ask him.

He just shrugs and nods. "Okay, " I hop off of my car and he does the same "I will see you tomorrow." "Yeah." He starts to open his car and I walk up to him and hug him. "Really thank you, for also helping me with the anxiety attack." He hugs me back and we stay there for a few seconds.

He pulls away and gets in his car.

***

I am home now in my bed. I can't sleep, I'm thinking about what happened in the last few hours.

Asher is not who everybody says he is.

I think for a while then drift off.

_____

Authors note!!

Asher and Ana are getting closer!!!

But will Asher let let her in?

ch 14

It has been 2 weeks since everything has happened. Loren is better, my mom has been seeing her new boyfriend, Violet has been with Nate so I haven't really hung out with her, and Asher and I have been getting along pretty well.

A couple of days ago Asher and I went to the beach and turns out he is a great listener. Problem is..I don't know much about him, we always talk about me and he is always helping me but I still know nothing about him.

Right now I am on Spring break which means no school for 2 weeks!

I'll thank the universe for that.

It's Monday and I have nothing to do and no one to hang out with so I decide on going on a walk around the city but first, iced coffee and breakfast.

I drive around to check out any new cafes in the area and after about 5 minutes of driving, I see one. It's a small brick cafe with black and white.

Talk about aesthetic.

Walking into a cafe was like walking into the happiest place on earth. Everyone in is was smiling and the employees were all laughing.

The inside was just as stunning as the outside but a bit better. There were plants, paintings, and decorative things to compliment the black and white theme. This is definitely going to become one of my favorite places.

I go up to the front counter and look at the menu. "Take your time!" The lady at the cash register said smiling.

She was a bit shorter than me but not by much, and her smile was contagious. "You know what, surprise me," I say with a smile on return.

I look around to find a place to sit and I see a small table in the corner with plants surrounding it and a big window right in front of it.

It is a table for 2 so I feel just a bit awkward because I'm alone. I was caught off guard by a very cute boy walking into the cafe. My jaw dropped. He had blonde hair, blue eyes, nice lips, and a pearly white smile.

The boy takes his order then finds a place to sit.

I look back down and just go on my phone. Don't want to seem like a creep. I hear someone get in the seat in front of me.

I slowly look up and my jaw drops to the floor this time. It's the boy.

I smile and do an awkward wave. "Hey. I saw you looking at me and you seemed pretty approachable." He says, and boy let me tell you his voice was PRETTY.

I smile and laugh a bit. "Thanks?" I say more like a question. He nods as a 'you're welcome' response.

The lady comes with our orders. "Thank you..?" I say. "It's Mia." "Well, thank you, Mia, you have a pretty name by the way!" She turns a bright shade of red. "Th-thank you." She smiles and walks away. "Well isn't she adorable." The guy says. "Very."

"Umm. I never got your name?" He looks at me. "It's Logan." I nod.

He looks at me expectantly and I raise an eyebrow. "And yours...?" He says slowly and sarcastically. I playful roll my eyes, "it's Anastasia." He looks at me and it appears that he is thinking about something.

"I'm going to call you. Hm.. " he slowly taps his finger on his sharp chin.

All of a sudden his face lights up. "I'm going to call you hazel!" I look at him dumbfounded. "Why hazel?" I take a sip out of my coffee. "It's your eye color, which by the way, you have very gorgeous eyes."

Oh God, I can feel my face heating up. I stopped the blush before it came.

After about an hour or so of sitting down and talking, I learned some interesting things about him. He and his family moved here from London, he loves vanilla ice cream, plays the piano, is basically rich and is moving to my school. In my opinion, he is very formal.

"Hey I am going on a walk around the city today and since I am going alone I was wondering if maybe you would want to-" "I would love to go." He cut me off and I give a smile whole receiving one.

I give a 20$ tip to Mia and I ask her for her phone number.

After exchanging numbers, Logan and I head out. I keep my car parked here since it's in the middle of the city and around everything.

The sun is hitting the area just right. I take a deep breath "you ready?" I ask him. "Ooh yeah." He says in a manly voice which causes me to burst out laughing.

***

We have been walking around for about 40 minutes and I swear we have visited almost every single store in New York City. "Oh please no more, I think I just might die." He says over dramatically and putting the back of his hand on his forehead, which again, causes me to laugh.

We both bought a few knick-knacks here and there. After just a while longer, it was time to head back. By now it was 6 pm.

**

"See you later, yeah?" Logan asks. I nod "Yeah." We exchange numbers and he gets into his driver's car.

My mom and I have good ass money but not THAT good.

My car is just 1 more block down to the cafe, so I start walking again. The sun is starting to go down and the lights are starting to fill the area. Today was a good day. I think of myself.

I was almost to my car when I spot Loren and Violet hanging out.

Gosh, way to leave me out. I shrug and kept walking.

In my car, I go in and drive. Home doesn't really seem fun right now so I take a trip to the mall.

**

I'm in the middle of shopping for new clothes when I see Asher. When he sees me look at him I smile and wave my usual wave. Weird thing is, he doesn't wave back or smile back. What the hell?

I shrug and continue looking around.

I continue shopping and found some really cute things which I will be so wearing back to school.

**

I am home now and I'm thinking of pulling an all-nighter.

Yeah, might as well do it.

I gather snacks and blankets and turn on my tv in my room. I binge-watch Riverdale all night.

Authors note!

What is going on? Why is everyone ignoring Ana?

ch 15

We are already halfway through spring break and I have done absolutely nothing. My mom has gone back to whoever and wherever she was before and I am alone at my house.

So far spring break has been nothing fun which is as sad at it seems.

Another no plans day passes by and I'm on my porch sitting on the hanging chair.

I reminisce freshman year when I was in volleyball, had a boyfriend and so many other great friends. Speaking of vollcyball, that is what I should do today.

I shoot a text to Violet.

Me- hey! just wondering if you wanna hang and play volleyball?

Violet- hey umm.. can we play later? I'm kind of busy.

Me- oh yeah sure!

I put my phone down and sigh. So much for best friend huh? I decide to go to the volleyball gym anyways.

When I get there, I see Mia from the cafe I went to about a week ago. She is in one of the personal gyms practicing her spike and let me tell you, she has one good hit.

I walk in, "Mind if I join?" Seeing that I caught her off guard she almost stumbles back. "Oh hey! Yes of course." She says smiling.

We practice serving, setting, spiking, setting, and diving, you name it, we did it.

It has been 3 hours and we are sweating our asses off.

Mia heads to the shower room and we say our goodbyes. I feel odd taking showers here so I just take one at home.

***

After about an hour of showering, I feel great. I go inside my closet to find an outfit to wear because today I think I'm just going to pamper myself.

I threw on a simple black dress, a cardigan, and white air forces. The drive to the beauty salon was short and fun. My music was all the way up and my windows we're down with me screaming my lungs out to the songs that played.

Today was my day.

**

When I enter the salon I get greeted by the women. Most people here know me because I often visit.

I get a facial, wax, hair treatment, now I am getting my nails done. As much as I wish V was here with me, she is probably busy.

So after I'm done i decide to give Asher a call. He picks up after the 3rd ring.

Me- hey! I was wondering if you wanted to hang out?

Asher- um..yeah sure i guess.

Me- sweet, I'll pick you up?

Asher- yeah sure just let me text you my address.

He then hangs up and texts me his address. But before I pick him up, I get snacks from the grocery store.

**

I'm on my way to his house. When I am here I am shocked at the size of it.

They have a 3 car garage, 3 stories and huge fountains in front of it.

My jaw drops to the floor. I see as Asher walk out and let me tell you, he looks good.

He opens the door "Hey." I say, but no words come out of his mouth. "Umm, where to?" I ask but once again no words.

"Okay, I'll choose. By the way, I got a lot of snacks and-"

"Who was that boy you were with yesterday?"

He caught me off-guard with that question, he also cut me off. "His name is Logan, I met him yesterday, he is new." He nods.

"Let's go." He says. What the fuck just happened?

***

We both went back to my house and watched movies for hours. Eventually, my mom called and told me she wasn't coming home for about a week. I just decided to he happy for her.

**

It's now 5 in the evening and I am about to make some dinner. I decide on making a simple chicken salad with water. Just healthy things.

"Not bad Smith." I roll my eyes playfully and throw a throw pillow at him which causes one to come plunging at my face afterward. "Oh, it's on." I competitively say with a grin.

***

My house is a mess with pillows all over it. Tonight was one of the good nights for the books. I got some pictures of me and Asher which are so going up on my wall.

Asher is so heartless around others but when I am with him I see a completely different side of him. A sweet and caring side. Everyone thinks he is so heartless, he isn't.

You are one odd human being Johnson.

Authors note

Nothing like teen love am I right?

ch 16

Violet's POV-

I know Ana thinks I'm ignoring her or leaving her out. But really I am just throwing her a surprise party and I suck at lying to her so I have to keep my distance until then.

Loren and I have been planning this for a few days now and when we saw her walking around with Logan we freaked out.

How do I know Logan? Well, he is my cousin. He is literally the definition of formal but he is super sweet and caring. I definitely think Ana and Logan should give it a try because they would be CUTE TOGETHER.

Today Loren and I are having a meeting today and we still have to rent a penthouse downtown. How do we have this money? Well, we live in Seattle so how can we not have this type of money?

The meeting is at 3 and it is 12 am. Loren is getting ready for a meeting with the party planner and I am making breakfast.

Ana does not like surprises but. She will LOVE THIS ONE.

***

"So here is a list of things we will need to make this a great party for your friends!" Claire the party planner said all cheery like. We both eagerly nod.

While driving to the store, I get a call from Ana asking if I can practice volleyball with her. Being away from her is making me sad but I need this to be an epic birthday for her.

She has been through a shit ton of stuff already.

***

After spending a massive amount of money, we both head to the local bakery and customize and plan the cake we want for her.

Anastasia is a sucker for chocolate cake.

The cake is 5 layers with frosting in the middle of each, and the decor for the cake is so pretty.

**

The day passes and we get more and more things done. I paid for this card store to make fancy invites. We only have 4 DAYS to get all of this ready.

It's going to be a long 4 days.

Authors more

Shortest chapter but it's a fill in :)

ch 17

Asher's POV-

Spring break is almost over. Kinda stupid.

Today I'm going to the beach with Abigail because she wants to hang out with her friends.

We were inside the car when a random question of mine popped up.

"Abigail, did you know Ryder Smith?" She looks at me wide-eyed and starts tearing up. "He-he was the only one that was nice to me." I stop at a gas station and give her a hug while stroking her hair.

"We will go inside and get all the snacks you want, okay?" She nods and wipes her tears.

Should I tell Ana this... No.

***

The girl at the cashier looks my age and she is being annoyed. She is bending at an angle so I can see her breast.

Does she think I'm new to this bullshit?

***

"That girl likes you." Abi giggles. I playfully roll my eyes and nudge her head ruining her hair.

At this point she is laughing so damn hard she can barely breathe.

The car roars along with Abi, "You ready munch?" She looks at me and nods her head.

Off we go to the beach.

***

Abigail is helping me set up the blanket and snacks. "Can I have snacks now?" Pouting her lips. I just nod.

I stick the umbrella in the ground and being out of the water bottles from my car.

"All set," I say. "Yay." She laughs and skips over.

We both stop and look at the puppy a little boy around her age is carrying. She giggles and runs up to it. "Puppy puppy!" Her hands high up in the air.

"Can I pet it please." Holding her hands together and begging. "Yeah, you can."

"Let's play!" The little boy nods and they walk up to make sandcastles and shit.

I go back to our area and watch them. I look around the beach and see a girl around my age. The girl looks at me and smiles with a shy wave. I smile, reminds me of Anastasia.

This girl is tall, blonde, blue eyes, a nice body, and she has the same exact look as the little boy Abi is playing with. I'm guessing that is her little brother.

"Hey!" She smiles big. "Hi," I say coldly. She is a bit taken back but I tend not to care.

Back to the heartless Asher, I go. "What is your name?" She asks. I shrug in response.

I turn to the beach and put my sunglasses on. "Oh, come on let's have fun." She says seductively. "Look, your little seduce shit doesn't work on me so scram." She rolls her she's and stomps away.

***

3 hours pass. Abi is still playing with the little boy and that girl is staring at me nonstop. I roll my eyes and flip her off not caring enough to look at her.

The sun was setting and I was ready to go home. "Abi, we have to go now!" I yell.

She gets up and wipes the sand off her and says bye to the boy and his puppy.

THE NEXT MORNING

It's 1 in the afternoon and I just some up. I got no plans today so I decided to just say home.

My phone rang and the number is unknown but I answer it anyway.

Me- who is this

Unknown- hey it's violet, i need your help mister

I roll my eyes.

Me- hell no i don't-

Violet- no wait please, Anastasia's birthday is in 3 days and i need help setting it up. She won't get too suspicious, i think she forgot her birthday.

What the hell, Ana's birthday is in 3 days and no one told me till now?

Me- fine. Text me where to go.

I then hang up, get the text, and get ready.

My phone lights up.

Violet- oh also bring snacks u miserable barbarian

I sigh and grunt.

Whole Foods is packed with people today what the hell.

I head over to the area of the chips and grab whatever I see, along with, candy, cookies, gum, gummies, I literally bought the whole snack section.

The penthouse was definitely huge. The windows filled up the walls, the kitchen was modern, the couches we're different, the whole place gives off a chill vibe for sure.

I kinda like it.

"Hey grumpy, give me the snacks." I grab the big bags that have the snacks in them and hand em over. "I told you to bring snacks, not the whole damn store!" I roll my eyes and plunge down on the couch.

"Are you and Ana like..." she asks as she looks at me expectantly.

I shake my head no. "Oh come.on, you both like each other it's so obvious. You guys just don't know it yet. It's all hidden feelings." I look at her then lean my head back, close my eyes, and think.

Do I like Anastasia? No, we are just friends. I don't date. Love isn't real. Relationships don't last.

"Loren help me set these up. Asher do you know what the plan is?" I look up, "No."

"Okay so I will find a way to get Ana over here and when she opens the door, obviously everyone yells surprise. Her close friends will be spending the night here, so that means you too. There is a pool in the backs and the volleyball gym is downstairs. Let's all hope she loves it." I look at her in shock. "All that for a birthday?" I ask. She rolls her eyes and sets up the streamers.

....

"Yay Ashy is home!" Abi calls from across the hall. I laugh and hold my arms out. She comes running and jumps into my arms. "Let's go watch a movie!"

I set up the TV and get snacks from the kitchen. When I walk back, Abi is choosing a movie. Smart for a 7-year-old.

We decided to watch Moana since she adores that movie. While she watches, I space off thinking about what Violet said today.

I don't like Anastasia.

I carry Abigail up to her room since she is already fast asleep. I then proceed to walk back downstairs and grab my phone on the couch to make a call.

Hey, dude, can you meet me and a broken bridge?

Yeah sure man, see you in 10.

"So you basically came here to tell me that you don't know your feelings or what feelings are?' I stare at him a little angry because yeah, how do feelings work?

'Maybe you don't, maybe you do. Maybe it's hidden feelings man."

"Funny, that's what your little girlfriend told me," I say with a chuckle. "Let me guess, she made you help with the party?" I roll my eyes and sigh dramatically.

...

I'm in bed thinking about how my unknown feelings towards Anastasia.

I. Don't. Like. Her.

Authors note

Hidden feelings

ch 18

Anastasia's POV-

Today I woke up and just wanted to stay in bed.

School is in a few days and I am not all that excited. My mom got a new job and works with the CEO of a big company and she is making so much money.

I am thinking of getting a job, to keep me occupied.

It's 2 in the afternoon and I am downright bored.

The weather is not the best today so the beach wasn't an option. Maybe I could go to the gym?

The gym is full of sweaty guys carrying heavyweights. Yeah sure there are a few girls here but they were kinda unnoticed. I took my jacket off and had my sports bra and leggings on. One guy whistles at me.

Rolling my eyes, I decide to pay for one of the personal rooms instead of work out in front of creepy guys.

The rooms were a little HUGE for 1 person but oh well.

I wouldn't necessarily say I'm weak, but I wouldn't say I'm strong either. Full-body workouts are a must. Going to the gym and exercising is not hard for me. It's a coping method quite honestly.

The gym was satisfactory. I spent 3 hours there, longer than usual.

Now I am heading to whole foods and getting some things for dinner.

I only eat healthy unless it's one of my cheat days. Today is not sad, so, I get a few vegetables and vegan noodles.

The last at the cashier appeared extremely miserable with a tad bit of sad. Because of that, I give her a 100$ dollar tip and the look on her eyes after warmed me.

It is my mon's money, not mine and I don't want it but she gives it to me anyway.

Others could use the money more than me.

The grocery bags were taking up my whole trunk. When I go to the store, I always ending up buying more than I need.

Its was 6 in the evening and I was nearly about to make dinner. I get all the ingredients out of the bags to begin the making.

Vegan pasta is one of my favorite dishes. Although, no one makes it better than my dad. I place the plates and silverware onto the table and put the pasta on 2 sets of plates.

The smell of it made me happy.

"Oh honey, thank you. Let's eat shall we?" My mom told me. "We shall."

She gave out a satisfactory "mmm." I laughed a bit. She seemed happy.

I'm in the shower with a towel wrapped around my body and hair, shaving. I accidentally cut myself with the razor. I roll my eyes in annoyance and keep going.

When I am done I dry off and change into sweats and an oversized t-shirt. Maybe I should go to the broken bridge? I nod my head.

I found that going to the broken bridge at night has become one of my favorite things to do.

I sat there admiring how beautiful the stars twinkled in the sky. Tonight was a full moon and it certainly lit up the dark.

I sigh. The night got colder as the time passes.

I don't want to do anything tomorrow.

After thinking about tomorrow, I wondered if Violet had forgotten my birthday. I mean, I did.

I didn't remember till now.

I thought about my birthday last year.

*** F L A S H B A C K ***

"Good morning sweetie!" My dad half-shouted, "Happy 16th Birthday!" He proceeded to hug me "Oh sweetie, your growing up so fast." My mom said in a sad tone while hugging me.

"RAWRRR" I get frightened with Ryder's little surprise in his hand. "Happy birthday Ana! I got you a present!" He handed me a small box, my eyes catch a glimpse of the bracelet inside.

Its black and white friendship bracelet with the words saying 'best sister ever' on it. I almost shed a tear.

Slowly, I bend down to his height and give him the biggest hug with a little nuggie on the head. "Hey!" He laughs.

E N D O F F L A S H B A C K

I didn't realize I was crying until I felt the collar of my sweatshirt. I try to stop crying but I can't.

I miss my dad. I miss Ryder. Life is shitty without them. I wish-

My thoughts are interrupted by a phone call.

Me- Violet, hey?

I tried my absolute best to not break down while on call.

V- hey tomorrow I need you to meet me somewhere to talk. It is important. I'll send you the address in the morning. Good Night.

Strange, I think to myself. I figured it was time to go back home. I get in my car and drive home.

The moment I smash into my pillow,

it was sleepy time for me.

***

I woke up at an unusual time but I couldn't go back to sleep. Birthday jitters maybe? Today I took time to get ready, plus I was meeting Violet at this place, she hadn't texted me the deets yet.

I take a shower, brush my teeth, do my makeup, and so on. "Honey, I need you!" My mom calls from downstairs. "Coming!" I walk downstairs to are my mom with a box in her hand. "You're up early," I say with a small chuckle. "It's your birthday, remember?" I nod.

"Well, here is one of your gifts." She places a small box in my hand. I slowly open the box and I almost drop dead when I see what's inside. "No, you didn't!" I scream. "Oh yes, I did." My mom grins and winks at me.

I run as fast as I can outside as I stare in awe at what is in our driveway. It was a white, matte, Lamborghini.

My dream car. I look at my mom, not saying a word, I hug her.

***

Asher's POV-

Today was the day. It's 6 in the morning and I am meeting up with Violet, Loren, and Nate at the penthouse.

First, I go to the store to get all the munchies for the party.

Then I go to the mall to get her a present. Problem is... I have no idea what to get her.

I probably should have thought of that before but whatever.

Violet sent a text to everybody.

hey guys. i was on call with ana yesterday and it was easy to tell she was crying. lets really try to make this day her best.

Everyone but me replied with a 'yeah!'

I look around everywhere not finding anything good enough for Anastasia.

Hours passed by and I finally find the perfect thing to get her.

At the penthouse, I am surprised to see I think his name is Logan? He was the guy that was with Anastasia about a week and a half ago.

We all start making final touches.

The party starts at around 7 and Ana comes at 8. Violet made expensive ass looking invites so I'm sure people are drawn to the party. Plus, it's in a big ass building.

It's now 7:58 and people already filled up the room. Violet saw Anastasia pull up in her new car I'm guessing.

I smile at the fact she has the same car as me.

Violet whisper yells firmly at everybody to "shut the fuck up and hide."

Mean much?

***

Anastasia's POV-

I slowly make my way up the stairs and open the door of the room number Violet gave me.

"SURPRISE!" I walk in to see a load of familiar faces jumping from different parts of the room.

I look at everyone in complete shock.

I think I was paralyzed for a split second.

I turn red at the thought of everyone looking at me. "Happy Birthday Anastasia Ryana Smith!"

"Oh gosh, thank you, V!" For a second I thought you forgot!" I said embarrassed.

She playfully rolled her eyes, "girl if anyone forgot about your birthday, it's you." I giggle.

I look around the room and my eyes land on Asher. I smile softly.

He returns the motion.

***

Everyone was drinking and having a good time. Violet really knows how to plan a party.

Everyone was with whoever and I am taking the time to walk around and explore this huge place. I walk upstairs to see the bedrooms.

There were 3 bedrooms. Each one was huge.

They all had king-sized beds, huge bathrooms that overlooked the city, a gigantic chandelier on the ceiling, and huge windows that filled the room will the lights of the sunset.

I look at the room in awe.

"Hello, pretty lady!" I slowly turn around to see Logan. "Logan, hey!" I give him a small hug. "Nice party isn't it?" I nod my head.

"So listen, one of your friends has caught my eyes. Ya know, blonde hair, blue eyes, shortish, and has a pretty eye-catching a smile." I gasp.

"You like Loren!" I yell. "Quiet there pretty lady." I lowered my voice. "You like Loren!" I whisper shouted.

I can see his face turning a light shade of pink as he tries to hide it. "Oh, that is definitely happening." I wink and proceed to make my way downstairs.

My eyes catch a glance at the huge food bar that is in front of me. I think I moaned at the right of the big chocolate fountain.

Violet really went all out.

I get a strawberry and dip it into the chocolate. Again I moan. "Did you just moan?" I hear a voice behind me.

I stop and stare in front of me as I felt my face flush red. "Uh..no." I declared, slowly turning around.

Asher.

"How do you like the party?" He asks curiously. "I love it, " I look around in amazement "I also love whoever picked out the snacks."

Right when those words left my mouth, he plastered a wicked grin on his face. I look at him, questioning as to why he is grinning. "So you love me huh?" Once again I could feel my face heating up at his words. "No no no no," I say.

I slowly back away and laugh.

I then try and find Violet to see what the plans are for the rest of the night.

After she explained to me the plans I ask "Who is sharing with who because there are only 3 bedrooms." She smirks. "Guess we just have to see huh?" She turns on her heels and walks over and kisses Nate.

I stand here dumbfounded.

I was. 'VIOLET!'

I know what she is really trying to do.

***

The party died down and there are only a few more people left. Some are helping clean and the others are standing around and talking. I, on the other hand, has done the most cleaning. These are loads of dishes to wash.

***

The place is cleaned up and all the hundreds of bodies in it. It's just myself, Asher, Loren, Violet, Nate, and Logan.

"So you all are wondering who is sleeping with who." I nod. "Logan and Loren will be sharing, " they both looked at each other and turned a slight shade of pink.

So cute."Nate and I will be sharing, " Nate then wraps his arms around her, "which leaves you and grumpy." Asher rolls his eyes. "God, would you stop calling me that?"

I look at Asher nervously. "You can have the bedroom, I think I'll sleep on the couch." He rolls his eyes. "Are you stupid? It's your birthday. Shouldn't you have a bed?"

Instead of discussing it, we all stayed up late to watch movies. Everyone was cuddling beside myself and Asher. It was a bit awkward but I didn't mind.

There were times where I swore he was going to put his arm over me but something stopped him every time.

I will admit over the past few weeks of knowing him, feelings started to develop. There is no doubt in mind that there was SOMETHING there. I think Violet knew that before I did.

But I can't do relationships.

Do I want him? I think.

Should I want him though? I'm not sure.

I stand up, "I'll be right back." I say to everyone. I make my way upstairs and plop down on the bed. I text Violet and Loren to come upstairs with me.

Not long passes till they are in the room.

...

'I think it's easy to tell you both have no idea what to do. You both are broken souls.'

***

Asher's POV-

'You two are broken souls man.' Nate says.

'She told me about her first break up man. Her mentality and heart are fucked.'

I sigh and shrug.

I catch sight of all 3 of the girls coming back downstairs. Right before they sat down I hear Logan say 'do why feels right.'

Everyone sat back where they were and everybody was hand in hand once again.

'Fuck it.' I mumble and wrap my hand over Anastasia's stomach and pull her closer to me.

With one arm over her and the other on her thigh that is over my leg.

***

Anastasia's POV-

The girls and I sat down in the spots we were at before. Someone unpaused the movie.

Befor I know it, Asher snakes around me and pulls me closer.

I swing my leg over his and one arm was over me and the other was resting on my thigh.

I couldn't help but have goosebumps. I look at the rest of them, they all were smirking.

Oh dear God.

All of us are cuddling someone now. Asher and I don't say a word to each other. He just runs his fingers through my hair while watching the movie.

Every once in a while I would look at the girls who seemed happy with who they were cuddling with.

It was nice.

***

Asher's POV-

I know this seemed like 5th-grade shit, but man this girl made me feel odd.

Having her in my arms felt nice, I think she enjoyed it too. She didn't notice I was looking at her the whole time she smiled at Violet and Loren.

The 2 girls look at me and mouthed "finally." I roll my eyes and pull Ana closer.

I didn't say anything when I wrapped my arms around her but neither did she. It was a comfortable silence. Nothing awkward.

***

Anastasi's POV-

1..2..3 movies later, it seemed like the others began to get tired.

Nate and Violet went to their room, then Logan and Loren, which leaves me and Asher downstairs alone.

I was laying on my back with my head resting on his lap facing towards him. I smile at him while he watched the TV.

"Take a picture it lasts longer." He smirks still not looking at me.

I roll my eyes and get up to go upstairs but again, 2 pairs of arms wrapped around me and held me close, once again.

"Let's go up now?" I asked. "I'm not that tired, but if you are, sure let's go." I frown when he doesn't look.

Of course, I'm tired but I will stay up.

"Let's watch another movie shall we?" He smiles softly and picks me up. I yelp.

"I know you are tired, let's go to bed." I smile and wrap my arms around his neck with my head leaning on his chest.

We get upstairs and he sets me on the bed and puts the blankets over me. I was still in my day clothes but I was too tired to care.

I see him walk over and lay down on the couch.

Guilt shot right through me.

"Would you in, like to sleep with me?" I ask knowing my face was red for the 3rd time, red. He smirks and gets up.

He walks over to me and gets dangerously close to my face. I start to feel shivers. "Goodnight, birthday girl."

I smile. He lays on the other side of the bed. I scoot towards him and wrap my body around his. He pulls me closer, closing the distance between us.

He runs his fingers through my hair until I fall asleep.

_____

Crazyyyyyyyyy shit

ch 18

Anastasia's POV-

A couple of days of hanging out with Asher have been pretty good. We have been hanging out so much more and the rest of girls are with their guys too.

Anyways, I am I'm 2nd period waiting for 3rd.

"May I go to my locker, please?" I ask the teacher. She nods and lets me go.

I was falling asleep, maybe a walk would help me wake up.

As I was walking, I hear a girl moaning. Ew.

"Meredith, we are going to get caught." When I heard who said that, my heart stopped for a moment.

I was towards the direction of the sounds.

I couldn't bear seeing what's right in front of me.

Asher and Meredith are basically swallowing each other whole.

I clap slowly and scoff. 'Low move Johnson. Fuck you.'

He smirks.

I then turn on my heels and walk away.

It may look like I'm not hurt, but I think my heart just took its maximum capacity of hurt.

I feel my eyes watering but there is no way in hell I'm going to sob over a stupid boy.

Again.

Asher's POV-

Today I woke up this morning to my stepmom and dad separating. Abigail doesn't know what was going on so she didn't care.

It made me think.

If love does that to people, I don't want it.

Don't get me wrong, I like Ana. But I will never let love, destroy me again.

...

It's 2nd period and I met up with Mere to hookup. I needed it.

I needed to tell Anastasia to fuck off.

Last night was nothing. She is nothing.

"Hey, baby." She says seductively. I smirk.

I begin to kiss her.

It gets more heated by the second, but we can't have sex in a school hallway.

I hear footsteps.

Meredith let's out soft sounds. "Meredith, we are going to get caught," I said.

5 seconds later, we stop at the sound of someone clapping.

With a scoff, she begins saying.

'Low move Johnson. Fuck you.'

Seeing her tried to hide her hurt was stupid.

You don't fucking want her Asher.

Right when everything was going good, awe mannnn

ch 19

'They swallowed each other. Fuck it. They can have each other.'

I have been with Violet and Loren for the past couple of days. They slept over at my house for a bit.

My mom and the rest of them think I'm not okay. Literally, she somehow managed a vacation for me and the girls soon.

"I should have never let you get like that with him." Violet growls.

I wasn't all that heartbroken. I mean yea it hurt for a little but it's not like I'm in love with him.

I cringe at the thought of love. What an odd thing.

Asher's POV-

"Jesus man, you definitely fucked up, " Nate said. "Yeah, you gotta get your shit together if you want Ana." Logan scoffed.

"I don't want her."

They both looked at each other and scoffed. "Yeah... You can stop lying to yourself now.'

I roll my eyes at them both.

Logan and Nate have been hanging out with me for 3 days straight. They are cool I guess.

They both nag at me all the time and go on and on about how I want her, how I'm lying, how I messed up.

I literally don't care.

Anastasia's POV-

I need toughen up. This shit is so stupid.

I decide to get up and get dressed.

Why? For no reason. I think I might go out and have a fun day with my girls. We can maybe go to the fair or the spa.

"You guys wanna go to the fair?" They both look at me with their eyes full of excitement with an eager nod. "YES!" They squeal.

"You both already know where my closet is, look at what you want to wear." They rush to the closet and I laugh.

I go to my other closet full of my less fancy clothes and look around for a decent outfit to wear.

This is what I decide to wear. Nothing too fancy.

"Done!" They both say in unison.

We all head out the door and drive. "Lunch first or no?" V asks. "Lunch first," I say. Loren just agrees.

Sometimes I feel like Loren feels she is left out. I don't want that. Loren is one of my best friends now. I want her to feel like it.

"Hey, guys I found this cafe the other day, the case I met Logan at. It was super cute." I say. "Let's go!" Loren says, "I love cafes, they are so cute."

We arrive, get in, order, then take a seat. I take out my book that was in my bag and start to read. "Loren, can you read in your free time?" V asks Loren. "Hell no. I never read." Violet nods. "How the hell does she do...that?"

"Guys I can hear you. Shut up." I chuckle at them both. "Food is coming." Loren excitedly said.

I just got an iced coffee and avocado French toast with a salad on the side. Loren got a macchiato with eggs and toast. Violet got an iced coffee with pancakes. I can't have junk food, says my mom. She doesn't want me to be unhealthy.

....

"Girl I'll try to get you it."

Violet is trying to win a game to get me a giant bear that my eyes are gawking at.

"WE HAVE A WINNER!" The young man says at the booth. He rings the bell loud enough for everyone to hear, they are cheering and clapping at V.

Violet got the bear and I told her to keep it. We are now walking around trying to find a cool place to eat.

Loren starts going crazy when she sees cotton candy so we go to the little booth.

We all get pink cotton candy and Loren got a large stick.

"She must really love cotton candy," I said quiet enough for only V to hear. She laughs and nods.

An hour or two passes by us and for the last ride we decide to go on the Ferris wheel.

We are in line and just as we are about to go on I bump into someone I didn't want to see.

Asher.

"2 tickets please." He tells the guy.

'Yeah... Nevermind.' I tell them and walk away. I don't want to be self centered but I can't do this to myself again.

'God you are so selfish.' I hear him scoff.

I stop and I am eye twitching angry. Slowly, I turn around and my hand makes contact with his face.

'I'm selfish? Are you fucking KIDDING me? Weren't you the one who had your hand all fucking over me? And what for? You are a no good scum back. The ONLY selfish one here, is you.' I could see the veins in his arms pop out. He is angry but it isn't my problem. I look too good to do this.

I know I deserve better than what I have received.

Loren and Violet say sorry to Nate and Logan and stay with me.

I flip Asher off and we leave.

...

Right now we are at a different game stand.

'ANA! I didn't know you had such power in you woman.'

Loren and Violet are still shocked at what I did. I feel good.

Everything is good right now.

The rest of the night is just me and the girls laughing at each other and what happened.

Asher's POV

'Don't look at us man, you brought this upon yourself.'

God I wanted to fuck someone up.

I didn't do shit. She is a little bitch who is so self centered and loves attention.

I grab my phone out and make a call.

The boys shake their heads, disappointed they walk away.

...

I am in my room with Meredith making out. Might as well just fuck all my problems away.

As things were about to really go, I stop. I'm too frustrated.

'Leave.' I demand her.

'Awe but Ash-'

I punch a wall.

'I SAID LEAVE.' I yell at her and I have never seen Mere so scared before.

She obeys me and goes.

I sit on my bed with my fingers running through my hair.

I think back to when Anastasia saw me and Mere in the halls.

How she tried to hide hurt.

The way she walked away.

That was when I knew.

I wanted her.

She has brought be nothing but positive outcomes. Being around her is like a breath of fresh air.

I call Violet and Loren.

...

'I know I fucked up. Jesus fuck stop telling me that will you?'

Nate, Logan, Violet, and Loren are here basically scolding me.

Maybe I DID mess up but they are being a bunch of assholes.

'Shut up Asher. You know you are in deep, deep, deep shit. You are lucky she doesn't know where we are. She mentioned something about a bridge.'

Violet is angry.

I roll my eyes and plop down on my bed.

Immediately I get up.

'I know where she is.'

It's only 11 at night.

Anastasia is normally at the bridge at night time so I speed there.

Just ask I expected, there she was.

In the outfit she wore at the amusement park. I knew she was cold. It was freezing.

I park my car next to hers and she rolls her car and hopped of hers.

Quickly, I get out of my car and go to her.

'Wait.' I call out she doesn't answer. She continues to open her car.

'Anastasia...' she stops. 'please.'

I know I have been an asshole and she has the right to tell me to fuck off but all I needed was to let her know what she meant to me.

'I'm sorry. Okay? I fucked around with Meredith because I this is too hard. Anastasia I'm really trying to understand relationships and feelings. I just can't comprehend them. I have never...' I stopped both angry and terrified of letting anybody know my feelings.

Ana's POV

He stopped talking. It sounded like he was thinking.

Slowly, I turn around and walk over to him.

That was all I needed to hear.

A small smile was exchanged from the both of us and we hugged.

'If you aren't ready, that is okay Asher. I don't really know if I even want anything related to relationships.' looks like we have both been through damaging lifetimes.

'I know about.. Your ex.' He told me. I guess Nate tells this guy everything. I shrug it off and go back to my car.

'Friends?' I ask him. The look on his face was strange when I said that but he agreed.

Soon enough, I'm on my way home.

ch 20

Anastasia's POV-

"Girl c'mon!" Violet and Loren are literally begging on their knees for me to go to this huge party thing. "Live a little Ana. Don't spend all of your life cooped up in your luxurious room." Loren says.

I frown, slowly giving in.

She's right though. I need to live a little.

I roll my eyes and groan. "Fine. Okay." Loren squeals and Violet smirks.

"Where and when?" I ask. "Where? At Brody's house. When? Well uh...tonight." I almost cry when I find out I have to start getting ready.

Oh, if you are wondering who Brody is, he is Violet's half brother. Brody I hear has the best parties around.

"Okay girls, it's 7:13 and the party starts at 9 so we have time. A lot of it. Shall we?" I grin, "We shall."

I guess they already knew they would be going because they brought their outfits.

"Omg guys Brody just texted me and there is a 90's theme..." I light up. I love the 90's. It's all so plaid and chic.

"I have a lot of 90's inspired clothes in my closet so get digging." They run to my closet because we are running out of time. "Oh also, I have an outfit already!" I announce to them, then walk off.

I get my outfit on and do all the makeup and hair needs. I stick some lollypops in my back for that extra sass of the 90's vibe.

(HER OUTFIT)

▫I added my own bit of style to it also.

After about 30 minutes, V and Lor walk out with pants hanging low and a tight shirt that showed their skin in between the waistline and shirt. "Cute guys!" I cheerfully say. "Girl you look like a badass," Lor said matter of factly.

I smile.

"Oh crap. Yall its 8:57! We have to go." I playfully roll my eyes. "Being fashionably late is better."

The moment we stepped into the door we could smell alcohol and sweaty bodies.

We got here around 9:30 because we wanted to eat In-N-Out.

"Drink or no drink?" She asks me. I shake my head no.

I was the one driving anyway.

So far, it has been nothing but all 3 of us on the dance floor and Loren and Violet getting drunk.

I feel a pair of hands wrap around my waist. I gasp and turn around, ready to hurt someone.

"Whoa, feisty much?" I chuckle. "Seriously Ash? You scared me." He grins. "Ash huh? I'll call you…" He taps his chin, "I'll call you muffin." I can't help but laugh, "Muffin? Why muffin?"

He rolls his eyes. "Because you always order them." I nod. He has a point. "Now, dance with me muffin." He winks and spins me.

This 'friend' thing might be too hard for me to do.

I look over to my side, Loren and Violet are with their little boy toys.

It's going to be a good night.

We danced and talked for about 30 minutes. We got sweaty and tired so we sat down on the sofa.

"You guys wanna go get a drink?" Logan asks. Everyone says yes, except for me. "I'll be right back, okay?" I nod.

"Aren't you thriving," Meredith said behind me. I roll my eyes. "What the hell do you want?" I ask annoyed. She smirks and gives me a sarcastic shrug. "Maybe I want Asher. Maybe Logan. Oh, wait, no…maybe Nate?"

This psycho bitch.

"Mhm," I told her not caring to say anything else. She obviously gets angry because of that. "Believe me when I say this you little whore, Asher and you little friends are too good for you. Stick with the one's in the back where you belong.'

I scoff.

I see the others walking this way, I think Meredith saw them too. She lowered herself to my ear.

"Also...sorry not sorry your poor little brother and daddy died." That was just enough to make me throw her from behind the couch to on it.

My hand snaked around her through with my other gripping the couch. 'Listen here you little bitch.'

The look in her eyes heod fear. Good.

'Mention their name one more fucking time or so God help me I will slice your throat, rip every limb in your body, and hang your fucking head in my room.'

I let go and she gasped for air.

'Now, repeat what I just said.' I demand her.

She shook her head no.

My fist made contact with her right cheek.

'I said, repeat what I just said.'

I could feel her shaking under my touch.

'You said never to mention their names again.'

With a satisfied smirk, I look at her one last time and said 'Good girl.'

I didn't realize the crowd around me till I look up. Asher, Violet, Loren, Logan, and Nate looked horrified.

Maybe it was bad. Maybe I went too far. Maybe my dad and Ryder wouldn't have wanted that.

Fuck what did I do. I gather my things and run out. In the distance I could hear them calling my name.

I don't go to my car, I just keep walking. Brody's house is not that far from mine but I don't go to my house.

Instead, I walk to the Pizza Palace.

"Hi, can I order a medium pepperoni sausage pizza please?" The woman gets my order and I sit at a small booth.

I open my phone up, go to Instagram, and look at all the pictures of my family on my account. I tear slips but I quickly wipe it away.

My elbow is resting on the table with my leaning on my hand. I always bring my notebook with me so I take it out and start writing.

"Here you go, the sundae and your meal is on me so don't worry about paying, love." I look at her in shock. Why would she do that?

"Thank you...?" I ask expectantly. "It's Aspyn." I nod. "Well, thank you Aspyn." She smiles and walks away.

I ate a few slices, I mean, they weren't that big. I was ready to go but before I went i ripped out a piece of paper from my notebook and wrote down

Thank you, Aspyn. Today was not a good day and you showing kindness made me feel okay. You are an angel in disguise.

After I wrote that, I left a 100 dollar tip for her and set them both under the table salt.

I look around and find her. When I do I say thank you once again and leave. I peek in the window, she saw the note and the 100.

Her eyes traveled around the room to find me when she does, she mouths 'thank you'

I do a little courtesy, smile, and wave bye.

I did not realize how much messages I got from the others. Specifically from Asher and Violet.

I told them I was okay and that I am going to pick the girls up.

It's late and walking outside at this time is a risk. I speed walk my way over to where I came from.

Halfway there, I hear footsteps behind me. I begin to walk faster. Taking a glance behind me, I see a guy with a good on walking behind me. I lose it and just start running. I hear the person jogging too.

The wicked laugh escapes from the guy's mouth. I can feel my body start to shiver. I go even faster.

"GO AWAY!" I scream and then hear their jog then into a full run. "I'll get you little prick."

I never thought I could run so fast in my life. It felt like my legs were giving out but I fought to keep going.

Soon enough, I arrive at the party and quickly run inside. I run to a window and look outside. The guy is standing right outside on the sidewalk.

My hands trembling, my breathing is heavy. I need to breathe.

"Hey, hey, hey, are you okay? What happened?" I look at Asher completely horrified. It took me a minute to process what happened.

'There was someone-' he looked at me waiting for me to finish. 'chasing me. The man was chasing me. He is outside.' I whispered.

"Ana, no one is there." I quickly turn around to see no one. I scan the room I run outside to look once more.

There was absolutely no one but Ash and I.

The laugh.

I know who that laugh belongs to.

'The laugh. Asher the laugh. He laughed while chasing me. I know who it was.'

Quickly, I ran to my car and drove to the police station.

After I give them the description, name, date, everything they needed.

It was about 2 in the morning when I left the station.

Asher's pov

Nobody knew where Ana was.

All of us tried to contact her but no response.

The girls were too drunk to stay awake.

Logan, Nate, and I decide to let the girls sleep since they were all in my guest bedroom.

We decided to search everywhere.

....

It's two am. Still no Ana.

Finally my phone starts ringing.

'I am home. I'm sorry for causing everyone such panic. I was at the police station doing something about the guy who followed me.'

Not even caring that she worried everyone, I was relieved she was okay.

'Should I go there?' I ask her.

'Yes please.' she whispered.

I hang up and tell Nate and Logan everything.

...

I was Anastasia's room with her.

The room was full of art, posters, books. It was nice.

I see why Loren and Violet always talk about her closet.

'It is messy right now I'm sorry.' there was makeup all over the floor along with clothes and a...

Thong?

I don't tell her. I don't want to embarrass her.

So instead, I help her clean up the make up and other clothes.

The lights were shut, there was just enough moonlight to let everything in the room be seen. The make up on her face had been smeared from crying I'm guessing.

Letting out a sigh I grab her hand a bring her up from crouching on her floor to get makeup.

She was taken back but I just hug her. We both don't say anything, we just stand there. Silent.

It was nice.

The last time I received anything like this was right before my mom died.

I miss her but life goes on I guess.

'You will be okay.' I whisper.

Both of us pull away and I noticed she was tired so I picked her and brought her bed to sleep.

Just as I was about to leave she grabs my hand.

'Stay.' she whispered.

****

AUTHOR'S NOTE

I DIDN'T EDIT THIS GUYS SO THERE WILL BE A LOT MISTAKES.

ch 21

Laughter fills the air.

Bacon's, eggs, and French toast are what my mom and Asher cooked for breakfast.

"Mommmmmm!" I whine. Mom is currently telling my most embarrassing childhood memories with the literal world and I am not here for it. "Okay okay fine. No more." The fake sadness of hers made everyone laugh.

After an hour of stomach hurting laughs, I got ready and changed.

Someone knocks on the door.

I say, "Come in!" Loud enough for them to hear me.

It was Loren, Violet, Nate, and Logan.

'Hey guys...' they all look extremely tired.

It must be because of me. 'Come in, I will make you guys coffee.'

Before I go I tell them not to tell my mom why happened last night.

They all agreed to not worry her anymore.

Everybody was on my couch talking to my mom but I kinda just sat there. I really want to leave town.

School was going to we can't.

Once everybody was done, we all just head to my room. 'Do you guys want to do anything today?' I ask them.

They all look too tired to respond. I sigh and let them rest.

Walking to my closet I look through my clothes to see if what to wear. I just threw on a comfy outfit since the weather was still a bit cold.

The only one awake was Asher. Strange how everything turned out. Between us and the group.

Instead of staying home, I walk my way back downstairs to see my mom.

'Hey mom.'

Before anything else, she proceeds to ask about Asher.

'You know when I first saw Asher I was like 'Who the hell did my daughter bring inside of this house.' but I like him for you Anastasia.'

I laugh, 'PLEASE mom, we are just friends.'

I think.

You know what...

'Hey mom.. How do you feel about the group taking a road trip? Don't worry you can come so you don't have to worry, I won't drink or do drugs I pro-'

'Ana' she says but I still ramble on. 'ANA!' she laughs .

I finally stop.

'Yes. You guys can go. I will tell your school you guys have something import to go to. You know I can handle it.' I smile.

I try to stop myself from bursting out of a happy scream. I hug my mom and run upstairs.

Even though I feel terrible for making them all sleep so late... I throw pillows at them.

Asher had no idea why I was doing this but he laughs and just starts throwing pillows at them too.

'Guys...' no response, 'GUYS!' I yell.

They all groan in response. 'I have something very important to discuss.'

All of them skip the morning grumpy and put on poker faces.

'It's good! I promise.' I announce.

'Anastasia, go on with it alreadyyyy.' V drags her words. With a smirk I ask,

'Who wants to go on a road trip?'

Every single one of them pop up and it was pure excitement.

'So... That's a yes?' I ask.

'I think we ALL need a break from everything.' Loren says. We all agree and start to plan.

My duty is

Snacks.

...

I am at whole foods getting snacks and goodies.

There was a little girl looking at me I smile and wave.

I proceed to keep looking around to see if I want anything else.

"All set," I say to myself while turning to the cashier.

"Hello! How is your day?" I ask the grumpy lady in front of me.

"Good." I frown at her dry response. "You're very pretty," I tell her. I'm really trying to brighten her day.

"Thank you." A small smile escaped her lips.

"It will be 132.89$" I nod and hand her the money. I take one of the packs of Hershey kisses out of the bag and give them to her.

"Have a good day ma'am!" I told her. "You too, thank you for turning such a shitty day into a good one." I do a little nod with a small smile and waved bye.

I put all the bags into the trunk and drive off.

I went to Petite Cafe and got everyone their favorite drinks with a chocolate muffin.

I call Asher.

Hey, I'm on my way home.

I'll tell the others. Your mom went to work and we are sitting on the couch waiting.

Oh, shit ill be there as soon as I can. You guys can just do whatever.

Okay bye.

I hang up and drive home.

"I'm home you hooligans!" I shout out. They all let out groans. "Finally sis." Loren whines.

"I got you guys your favorite drinks so do not complain." They all jump up from the couch and steal the drinks from me.

I roll my eyes and laugh at their desperate actions and walks to the kitchen.

Taking the snacks out of the bag, I put them on the island till tonight.

"Okay guys, what do you want to do for the rest of the day?" They all shrug.

All of us are bored and have no plans for the day.

We all decide to just sleep so everyone is energized and ready to go.

I'm not tired and neither I Asher so we stay downstairs and watch movies.

My head was on his lap while my hands were fidgeting with his.

We are just friends.

I think

...

Finally the time comes to leave. I have no idea why we all decided to go at night but here we are.

My mom kisses me goodbye. I think she sees I'm getting better.

I'm happy she is getting better too.

I met her boyfriend! He is not THAT bad I mean, he can't beat dad but he is pretty sick.

I'm excited for the week ahead of us.

Authors note

Aghhh! A road trip? This is going to be so exciting.

Also, I'm very sorry it takes me 100 years to update. I have school and high school has a lot of assignments to do. And i do HOME SCHOOL YALL.

Anyways, enjoy hooligans.

ch 22

SONG RECOMMENDED FOR THIS CHAPTER ::::::wHo by zayn malikITS TRULY A MUST TO LISTEN TOTHIS SONG WHILE READING THIS CHAPTER.

We have absolutely NO idea where we are going. Right now I'm the one driving.

Loren and Violet were on their boyfriends laps. So cute.

Taking random turns and exits. We decided to see where life was going to take us.

Everybody was taking pictures and videos for the memories of us. Even though I was the one behind the steering wheel, I felt amazing.

Since they slept all day, they will be up all night. Asher seems to have something on his mind.

I decided to save my questions for later.

Everyone was laughing and singing along to the music I was playing.

wHo by Zayn.

Became our song.

Clearly I'm the one out of all of us with taste. I just laugh.

The nights began to roar at us. The world seemed so small compared to us.

I have found my people.

Nothing was better than this.

Than us.

It was all of us against the world.

I roll down my windows and top hood.

The wind bursted through got everyone really feeling powerful amongst ourselves.

Violet and Loren pop up into the top hood and shout

'NO ONE CAN STOP US.'

The boys poked their heads out of the window.

'ITS US AGAINST THE WORLD BABY.'

It felt like I was high above clouds, this is my life.

I'm in love with it.

I look at Asher.

I'm in love with him.

This chapter made me very emotional, I'm not sure why but I cried writing it.

I hope you enjoy.

ch 23

I cant believe im starting this book back uponce again, PLEASE reread,this chapter and the rest wont makeANY SENSEif u dont go back and read :(***

The road had no one on it but us.

Everyone had bunches of fun just screaming and yelling all the things we wanted to say. I have never had such a free night. So happy. So at home.

It has only been a couple hours and I have never felt so alive in my life.

Everyone was smiling. The sight was beautiful.

Asher decided to drive half way through so we switched.

I am now in the passenger seat next time him. We took my mom's mini van so the rest were in the trunk laying down since we put an air bed on it.

'Thank you.' he told me. With a smile, I just nod.

Everything felt so right. So real.

Only a month ago was I on the movie theater ground. Nate saved me from Meredith.

That is when I remembered, if Nate didn't switch the story, who did?

I look at Asher.

I decided not to ask since Nate and Asher were both too happy.

There was just the smallest smile sitting on his lips.

He is happy? I think so.

I hope so.

Asher's POV

Anastasia was riding and she seemed to be having so much fun. Everyone was good.

Screaming, shouting. It was truly just

Anastasia Nate, Loren, Logan and I.

No one else but us.

Everything felt so.. Right?

Anastasia was laughed and opened the windows.

Loren and Olivia go to the top window and shot

'ITS JUST US AGAINST THE WORLD'

The boys and I look at each other and laugh, we all poke our head through the windows and shout everything we could.

'NO ONE CAN STOP US.' All of us shout.

We repeat those words over and over again.

It was true. With all of us to get here, nobody could stop us.

My eyes make their way to Anastasia.

Maybe I can love her.

Maybe I do.

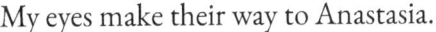

We have no idea how but we ended up in Oregon. It was 11 am. The sun was shining and everyone was fast asleep.

Anastasia laid on my lap to sleep while I was driving.

I was not tired despite being up for more than 24 hours.

Most my life had been sad and gloomy. My last is never something I talk about. It's full of lies and despair.

Soon enough, everyone starts to wake up.

The motions of the girl in my lap let me know she was awake.

Looking down at her and looking back at the road.

'Well good morning muffin.' Laughing at her, she groans and gets up.

'Asher Johnson I will kill you if you keep calling me that.' still laughing, the others go to their seats.

"I have no idea what turns I took or how we got here but... Welcome to Oregon everybody."

Anastasias POV

I feel bad Asher had not gotten any sleep. I woke up in his lap but he did not look not even a tad bit tired.

Everybody had so much excitement.

Who knows what the days will bring.

He told us we were in Oregon.

Huge buildings surrounded us and the sun was shining so good this morning.

'What shall we do today ladies and gents?' All of us think about it and decide we should get a hotel and find somewhere to eat breakfast.

I go on my phone to see a hotel we could stay at.

When I finally find one, I tell Asher the directions.

Just like the pictures, it was huge.

I already booked us a room of 3.

While everybody gets their things I go up to the receptionist and she tells us our room number.

I go back to them and tell them the room number and give them the 3 keys.

When all of us grab our things, someone goes and parks our car for us.

Thank God the boys are 18 or else we could not have done this.

The room was huge. Everyone already knew where they were sleeping.

Sheesh it was humongous. I already paid and booked our room but they don't know. Oh I really hope V doesn't kill me for this.

Everybody plopped down on the huge couch that was provided.

Our plan today was look around, take pictures, eat, sleep a little bit, then hit the road again.

I'm pretty sure all of us prefer the super late night drives. It brings life to us all.

Asher was focused on me and I didn't realize it. Feeling my cheeks heat up, I stop before they turn a red shade.

Instead of getting all shy, I decide to throw one of the couch pillows at his face.

'Anastasia Ryana Smith... You did not just hit me with a pillow.' he was shocked at first but the smirk on his face scared me.

Within a second I'm on the floor getting tickled. I could of sworn I was so, so close to peeing on the floor.

'Asher!' I call out begging for him to stop. I couldn't understand my own words with all the laughter.

Violet was taking a video of what was happening.

'No, no, no, no... AHH I'm going to die!' finally, Asher stopped tickling me. Catching my breath I give Violet a deadly look for taking a video.

With a rush, I push him onto the floor and start tickling him.

All of us were completely full of hysteria when we found out Asher was the most ticklish person.

It didn't last very long. Since he is much stronger than I am, he got on my and pinned my hands down with his own hands.

'I am so getting you back, Johnson.' He whispers in my ear. His face was only centimeters away.

I'm screaming inside.

The goosebumps were all over me. My heart was beating so fast and I could not stop my face from flushing this time.

He smirks with his eyes locked in mine as he slowly backs his face away from mine.

I can finally breathe again.

Everybody watched, not one person in the room didn't have a smirk on their face.

Red.Red.Red.

My cheeks we're hot.

Taking the pillows on the floor, I throw them at everybody.

Soon enough, it is just one big pillow fights.

Oh how bad I feel for the person who is going to clean this room.

Asher's POV

After I got off of her, her face flushed.

Violet got it on video, thank God.

Once our little pillow fight was done, I nudge Violet and she already knows what I was going to ask for.

The video.

We had a little discussion on the plans of today.

First, we eat.

Logan already found a place so we go to our car and drive to the restaurant.

'Holy shit.' Anastasia looks like she was in a gaze with where we were. Honestly, none of us expected it to be so high-class. I laughed at the fact that we were all still in our pajamas.

When we walked in we were greeted with a man with a suit and tie on and women with really, really tight dresses.

I think Anastasia was self conscious. Her eyes were on the lady right in front of me, her hands were holding her stomach. Suddenly, her head went down.

I didn't realize why she was acting that way till I noticed the lady in front of me was outing her for me. Bullshit like this always happened, especially with Meredith.

I don't understand why girls like them try to fuck with other girl's feelings.

My real mom taught me to never, ever hurt or allow that kind of behavior.

Of course, I had to throw my stone cold face at her and I snaked my arns around Ana.

'Table for 6.' I demand.

Just as expected, she puffed and left with an angry expression. I saw the others looking at me in shock. Instead of saying anything, my shoulders just did a small shrug.

There was no way I'm letting a try hard hurt Anastasia or any of the girls in our group.

Respect. They should learn it. A small voice in my head said. I scoff.

Anastasia's pov

When he snaked his hands around my waist, there were goosebumps all over me.

Why didn't he want that woman? She was beautiful with a perfect body.

Sighing to myself I just stay in Ash's arns and wait for the encounter to be over.

'Table for 6.'

Whoa, his voice was so cold. There was venom laced all around it.

My eyes land on the others and I give them a questioned look.

Looks like we were all confused as to why he suddenly went back to his old demeanor.

Soon enough, a different waitress comes. He smile cheered everyone up.

'Well isn't this a group of teenage love.' she said in awe. We all smile and giggle a little bit.

Asher's arns seemed to loosen around me which told me he was no longer angry at whatever he was angry about.

'Just follow me love birds.' the woman looked at me and winked.

What.........

The seats were in a more preserved area. I don't think we paid to be in this spot.

'Here are the menu's and I will be back in the blink if an eye with water for starters.' soon enough, she's gone.

Violet's pov

Asher and Anastasia seemed to be getting more intimate. I'm not against it, I'm just scared he is going to break Anastasia.

Again.

The girl has already been through hell and I don't think she has another heartbreak in her. I'm worried.

Ever since Asher has been with Ana, he changed but.. That doesn't mean he can't click into his old ways again.

Today showed me he was capable of still being such a cold-hearted teenage boy. For now, I'm just observing but..

I am truly rooting for them.

Loren's pov

Asher is completely different with Ana. Honestly, I think that girl has the power to bring out the best in everybody but herself.

But that is what Violet, Nate, Logan, Asher, and I are here for.

We are friends.

And I hope we are all friends forever.

It is strange feeling so loved.

I never really had it growing up.

Nate's pov

I have never seen Asher as happy as he is right now.

I mean, other than when he is with Abigail but that is it.

Anastasia is changing him and it's as clear as crystal to tell.

Whether he knows it or not, he likes her.

Maybe even loves her.

Logan's pov

Anastasia told me about her past. All of us know of it now but.. I hope Asher does not hurt her again. That is the last thing she needs right now.

That girl has been blooming recently and I am truly proud of her.

I'm also thankful she got me Loren.

This girl will truly be the death of me.

****

Hey! Did you guysLike that I putALL of their pov'sOr should I stick to justAsh and Ana?

ch 24

✱ **MATURE SCENE***

Ana's pov

We are back on the road after such a long day. We slept for around 6 hours and had fun the rest.

This time, Logan was driving and next is Loren.

Songs were playing and everybody sat in a comfortable silence. Asher and I were in the middle seats, V and Nate were in the back, and Loren and Logan were both in the front.

My head was leaning on the window looking at the sky.

These are the moments I wish I could stay in forever. Thinking about it, our senior year is next year. This school year only has a couple months left to it and I don't know anything about my future.

All I truly know is..

I don't want this friendship between all 6 of us to end.

It was special. To me as least.

***

Everyone was fast asleep but Logan and I.

'You look like you have something on your mind. You okay?' he asks me.

'Yeah, I'm fine. Just thinking.' he nods and focuses back on the road.

'Hey..' with a pause, I continue, 'what do you think it is going to look like for all of us after senior year?'

He sighs.

'Honestly, there is really no telling. All of us might never talk again. All of us might be friends till the coffins are 6 feet underground. Life is weird, I don't get it at all but, what I hope..' he stops talking.

His eyes land on mind through the mirror and back to the road.

After a few seconds with a deep breath, he proceeds.

'What I hope is that no matter where life takes us all, we stay together because...i don't think any of us will ever find a friendship so incredible.'

I don't say anything.

I bring my knees to my chest and rest my head against the seat.

This friendship has taught me so, so much.

It has only been a month. There is so much more I want to do, learn, and see with them. If it ends, if it ends...

Instead of finishing the thought I look outside. The city lights were beautiful at night. A dream, really.

'What all of us have, is worth fighting for.' Logan whispers.

Logan's pov

I understand why Anastasia is worried about all of us splitting.

Honestly, her and the girls are the glue to it all. To us.

Whether Asher wants to put his pride and ego higher, we all knows he wants her.

His past was not necessarily easy. Especially with love. Nate, Asher, and I were having a talk the night Asher told us he wanted help with Anastasia after he was caught with Meredith.

I felt bad for the guy. I would have ever guessed the things he had been through if he never told me.

Anastasia was looking outside the window.

'What all of us have, is worth fighting for.' I whisper to no one. Just a thought.

Just a month and we have all been through it with something.

I wouldn't have found Loren if it wasn't for Anastasia.

Nate wouldn't have been with Violet if it wasn't for Anastasia.

Asher would not be who he is right now if it wasn't for Anastasia.

Anastasia was something special to us all.

I am extremely grateful for her.

Everybody is.

Anastasia's pov

We ended up in California.

I have really wanted to go here so I am excited to spend my time here with my people.

'Guys c'mon! I'm hungry.' Violet kept rushing because

1. She really needed to pee2. She was hungry

'Violet, we are almost there woman. Chill out.' Nate played with her.

She huffed and whined.

I just laugh at how crazy she gets when she is hungry.

Asher playfully nudges me.

'What are you smiling about?'

I shrug and give him a smirk.

Instant regret.

He picked my up and threw me over his shoulder in front of EVERYBODY.

'Asher!' I couldn't stop laughing. Oh the embarrassment.

'What's the magic word?' Oh dear God.

'PLEASE!' I laugh.

'Errrr. Wrong.'

'Asher, do you not remember we are in a Mall. People probably think you are kidnapping her dumbass.' Violet and Loren were trying to help me out.

Finally, he puts me down and rests his shoulder on my head. Since I was smaller than him, it was his advantage.

My arms we're crossed our of utter humiliation.

'Oh come on, you are fine.' he plays around and puts his arm around me and pats me on the head.

'I'm not a baby.'

***

Finally, we got food. I was starting to get hungry too.

It was around 3 in the afternoon and we got tacos. My favorite.

The girls were talking about school. The boys were talking about the game they were going to miss.

Football made no sense to me. Violet makes fun of me for it but it's understandable.

I cheer so I will miss the game too. No regrets though, I'm having the time of my life.

'Hey guys, the food is here.' I tell them.

'Thank you!' I tell the waiter. He smiles and gives out the food.

The people in the restaurant were all teenagers around our age. There were two girls in the table next to us.

They were both gorgeous.

'Hey!' I call out to them. They both look at me, 'you guys are really pretty.'

They flash a smile and thank me.

Soon enough we all started to have a conversation with them.

'I'm Kyana and this is my girlfriend, Vicky.'

I thought it was so cool how they looked so perfect together.

Kyana had beautiful dark skin that glowed. Like.. Literary. Glowed.

Vicky was the opposite, her skin was pale and she had the brightest blue eyes. Her hair was almost white.

The afternoon was a long one. We stayed for a few hours just talking to them.

'We are from Oregon! We are down here for a cheer tournament right now. Hectic schedule but we are on the same cheer team. Varsity.'

Violet and I look at each other in excitement. 'We do cheer too! Both on Varsity. We cheer for football and basketball.'

'Awe that's so sick! We cheer for the girl's basketball team and the boy's football.' Vicky said.

These girls we're super cool.

***

After lunch we all exchanged numbers and hopes to see each other again. So far everything has been fine.

We were near a beach so we all decided to kill time there.

Instead of going to the crowded area, we were isolated off from the rest of the people.

'Anyone wanna go swimming?' Violet asks.

Me and my girls smirk at each other and strip down to just our under undergarments.

Running to the water we laugh and I push Violet down under. Loren does the same to me and Violet does the same to Loren.

I almost died, I was completely out of breath.

Soon enough, the boys come and join us.

'Finally!' I told them and splashed water at all of them.

Asher smirks and I know what he is about to do.

I try to run as fast as I could but it was no use..

I fell.

Asher snaked his arms around me and threw me in the water.

'You did not!'

'Oh, but yes I did.'

Now it was just one huge water fight against the girls and guys.

Honestly, I haven't had this much fun in almost a year.

'This is all the girl's fault.' Nate lectured.

'No it's not!'

Violet pushed him under the water. Be idea might I add.

Nate got on her back and wouldn't let go.

My legs were about to completely give out because I was laughing so hard.

***

Almost an hour has passed and we all got dressed into our clothes.

The boy's stayed shirtless so the girls and I stole then and put them on.

'Hotel to shower?' I asked.

After they all agree, we were ball to the hotel in no time.

Asher's pov

Everybody is in their rooms getting cleaned up.

Nate and Logan went out to go get snacks cause they were done already.

I think Violet and Loren went with them.

My mind was going fucking crazy.

I want Anastasia. I do.

I think.

But I don't want to do this love bullshit.

It's not real.

Fuck.

My hand ran through my hair.

Love isn't real

It's bullshit

Your dad proved it.

It's a lie.

You won't last with her.

You will fuck it up.

My mind was loud.

'Fuck.' I growl.

My first game in contact with the wall.

Only a few seconds later, someone game running into the door.

Anastasia.

Her breath was shaky and of course, she was worried.

She opened the shower door and her eyes were only on mine. Not looking down.

I had no clothes on.

Neither did she, there was a towel wrapped around her body.

Don't do it.

It's not real.

You will ruin her.

My mind was loud but I ignored it.

I kissed her.

Anastasia's pov

My towel dropped and I was in the shower with him.

Our lips collided. There was nothing I wanted more than him right now.

He growled under my lips.

His fingers traced my stomach and further down.

A moan cane out of me. Then another. And another.

'Asher.' I pant.

My back hit the wall and his hands held my firmly down.

His lips trailed all over me. Going down each second.

Another moan.

There was a bang on the door.

'Asher buddy-' it was Nate and Logan.

'Holy fuck-' Logan drops his bag and I hurriedly wrapped my towel back around my body.

My eyes were locked in Asher's.

'I'm sorry.' I tell them.

I run out and back to my room.

Violet's pov

'I almost had sex with Asher in the shower.'

Anastasia was out of breath and only wrapped in a towel.

I had no words.

'I don't know. It wasn't love. It was anger. He was frustrated about something. There was something on his mind the whole time.'

Her knees hit the floor.

Loren and I rushed over to her.

She was still soaked from the shower but her tears covered more of the floor than the water from her body.

'I-I think I was just his...'

'his..'

'distraction.'

ch 25

Anastasia's pov

'Asher!' I ran over to him laughing at the him. Logan and Nate were ruining his hair.

The trip was almost over. It has been around 4 days and today was the last one.

Violet, Loren, and I decided to spend a girls day and the boys had their own day too.

Instead of going to the mall like we normally planned, we met a girl named Mariah yesterday and invited us to her brother's party.

So, we all stayed at the hotel and waited for the time to get dressed which was in about an hour or so.

9:45

The party started at 12. Kind of late but who cares honestly.

'I'm gonna get ready now. I have nothing else to do.' without staying to hear them say anything, I bring my bag into the bathroom and put my clothes on.

My energy was drained already so the outfit that was originally planned wasn't gonna happen.

A white t-shirt, grey sweats, and nike air forces are fine.

Huh?

My phone rang.

'Hello?'

'Just came to say I won't be here when you come home tomorrow. I have a date with Derek!'

Yeah.. My mom has a boyfriend. I forgot.

'That's great mom. Have fun.'

A couple more words were shared then the call ended.

With a sigh, I get ready.

***

It's as you expected.

The music was blaring. The teenagers we're making our and grinding on each other. The lights were flashing. Red solo cups we're everything on the ground. The smell of alcohol and weed filled the air. Crazy party.

'Let's get wasted ladies.' Violet demanded. As much as I wanted to, I am the one who has to drive us all the way back home.

'No. I'm driving.'

'But-'

'Quit Violet.' I had to use a more firm tone because I know Violet would keep trying to persuade me.

Loren understood why I did not want to drink and I'm thankful for that.

Mariah came out of nowhere and put her arm around me. 'Hey.' she said.

The already wasted girl told us where everything was and where the bathrooms were. 'Thanks.'

'Well, no time to waste, let's go.' Mariah grabs my hand and tells the girl's to follow.

We ended up at a bar inside the house. V and Lor got shots but I planned on staying sober. They were drinking and I had my elbow on the table resting my head in my palm. Tonight was going to be a long one.

The girls grabbed my hand and took us all out to the dance floor. Loren and Violet dressed the part but I wasn't. And honestly, I didn't want to be here.

I'd rather be at home reading or at Hope's Cafe. Maybe I'm home sick. I don't know but, I miss my mom.

'I'm going pee.' with that, it was a trip to find the bathroom. The house was big but I'm sure it won't be that hard to find.

The hallways that I entered was dark and no one was in it. Moans cane out of most of the rooms and it made me uncomfortable.

Good news, I found a bathroom. Bad news, it was taken.

Mentally groaning, my fist slowly pushes up against the wall. Nothing feels right. Everything feels weird. I hate it. It has been like this since the shower incident with Asher.

He has never seen me completely undressed before. He touched and kissed me in places I loved but, it was for him. Not for me.

Can you tell I've been avoiding it. He does not know I know that he was using me as a toy in the moment. It was obvious.

Between each kiss, each lick, each bite, each moan. There was something on his mind. I don't understand. Was I really just his toy?

That was a question I would probably never get an answer to.

My back hit the wall and I sat down. Curling my knees up to my chest I close my eyes. The music was do loud you could feel the vibrations from the floor and in your chest.

Tired. Exhausted. Drowsy.

A couple ran out of the room laughing and hands on each other and in came a new one to go in the room. God everybody was horny.

Mentally groaning and getting off my ass, I slowly walk back to where Loren and Violet were.

They were dancing having fun. All eyes were on them. Why wouldn't they be? They are both gorgeous.

Instead of bugging them, I go off to the couch.

I knew this party wasn't going to be any fun for me. The only reason I went is because V and Lor wouldn't shut up about it.

Instead of moping about everything, I sat on the couch and did what I said I wouldn't do.

I moped.

'What got your panties in a bunch?' Violet and Loren came up to me. They were wasted. Couldn't even walk straight.

I just shrug.

'Stop being such a boring person and actually do something for once. You carry negative energy everywhere you go now. It is kind of annoying.'

As sad as her comment made me, I had to remember she was drunk. And so was Loren.

'For real Anastasia, Asher is Asher. He clearly does not want you. You are a toy to him.' Loren laughs in my face.

Ouch. That really hit a spot.

'Okay.' I tell myself and took a deep breath.

'Let's go guys. It is getting late.'

Literally 3 am.

'No. We don't want to go with you.' they argue.

'Guys please don't make a big fuss. Let's go.' I grab their hands and try to lead them to the front door.

They shove me to where I almost fall and once again, they laugh about it.

'Get Logan and Nate. We don't wanna go with you.'

Ouch again.

Sighing, I do what they say.

Making sure no one does anything to them, I sit and wait for Logan and Nate to come.

Which, not long after, they show up and take the girls back to the hotel.

Once I know the girls are safe, I go to my car and just sit there. There was no point in going to the hotel. Loren and Violet did not want me around right now.

Asher showed up on my ringer but I declined the call. I don't really feel like talking to anyone. There wasn't any point really.

Okay, maybe one person.

'Hey mom.' I couldn't hold the tears in.

'I really want to go home. I miss you. Nothing has been going good. This whole trip was shit. The girls don't even want me around right now. Am I really that dull? I'm really trying to stay together but-'

Lowering my voice to a mere whisper

'-but I can't.'

On the other line was a worried mom. I'm so thankful I have her.

'Okay. Baby, I know it is hard. If Loren and Violet want to be like that, then let them. See if they will cool down a bit before you talk to them. You guys have a special friendship, it will work out. I just know it will Ana. For now, just hang in there until you come home okay? I will be here waiting for you.'

I was sobbing. I couldn't talk right, my voice was so quiet.

'I love you. I love you so much.' I couldn't stay to hear her response.

Ending the call, I rest my head on the steering wheel and let my tears soak my clothes.

Why was everything going to wrong.

www.ingramcontent.com/pod-product-compliance
Lightning Source LLC
Chambersburg PA
CBHW072158070526
44585CB00015B/1204